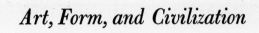

Art, Form, and Civilization

Art, Form, and Civilization

University of California Press
Berkeley and Los Angeles 1952

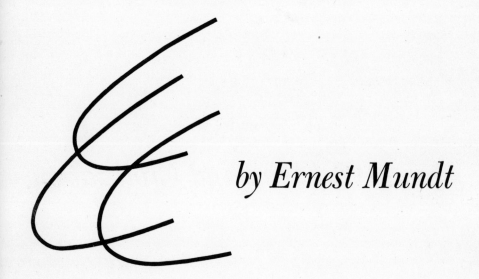

by Ernest Mundt

University of California Press
Berkeley and Los Angeles, California
Cambridge University Press, London, England
Copyright, 1952, by
The Regents of the University of California
Printed in the United States of America
Designed by John B. Goetz

Introduction

Western man is in search of a new synthesis. Civilization is losing order and meaning under the stress of forces that destroy through their lack of unitary aim. Research has outdistanced the development of a meaningful pattern for life. Analytical methods, although successful in many fields, have weakened the unity of ideas and have resulted in a specialization so intense that the common purpose of all knowledge—to help man embrace life more fully—is all but forgotten. The new synthesis would center on unitary man who, through harmonious interaction of his senses, his feelings, his intuition, and his reason, would relate himself to his fellow men, to nature, and to God. Instead there are economic man, political man, man the scientist, man the philosopher. Even religion has become a specialty. And so has art.

Today the dangers inherent in such overspecialization are all too evident. Men no longer naïvely cling to the optimistic belief in automatic, beneficial progress that was the inspiration of the nineteenth and early twentieth centuries. The recent war and its consequences have given rise to serious disillusion. In literature, from fiction to philosophy, there is repudiation of the former easy optimism, best summarized perhaps by Lewis Mumford in "The Condition of Man": "The period through which we are living presents itself as one of unmitigated confusion and disintegration: a period of paralyzing economic depressions, of unrestrained butcheries and enslavements, and of world-ravaging wars: a period whose evil fulfilments have betrayed all its beneficent promises."

At the same time, constructive ideas have been offered concerning the reasons for these catastrophies and the possibilities of transcending their vicious circle. Mr. Mumford finds these reasons in a breakdown of the over-all pattern of meaning and refers to Toynbee's "schism of the soul." Other writers, starting from different points of departure, have arrived at similar conclusions when they emphasize the need for integration. Erich Kahler in "Man the Measure," Reinhold Niebuhr in "The Nature and Destiny of Man," Lancelot Law Whyte in "The Next Development in Man," to mention three representative works on the rationalistic, theological, and biological levels, all insist that the compartmentalization of knowledge and consciousness must be overcome by some unitary idea emphasizing the essential oneness of all life.

Art has helped to effect such unification in the past; it is my belief that it has already begun to so function for the present.

For the ideas presented in this book I am deeply indebted to the late Professor Hans Poelzig, who has taught me the responsibility of the artist; and to the late Mr. Egon Friedell, whose studies of Western civilization have been an invaluable guide. I should like to express my profound gratitude to Miss Adelheide Pickert for her stimulating enthusiasm and intuition in matters of art.

Mrs. Cecilia Odefey Mundt has been a very real coauthor of this book. She has contributed her ideas, distilled from an inclusive experience with Western art and the social and human framework in which it has evolved. Her insight and awareness, knowledge and love, understanding, sense of justice, and critical objectivity have transformed my early sketches and have guided the book toward completion. To her go my very special thanks and dedication.

I am indebted to the Metropolitan Museum of Art, New York, for permission to use the photographs of portrait sculptures; to the New York Public Library for the reproductions of rare books; and to Mr. Frederic Prokosch for his kind permission to quote one of his poems. I should like to thank Mr. John Jennings for his patience and understanding in editing the text. I wish also to thank Mr. John Goetz for the craftsmanship shown in his design of this volume.

The drawings throughout are my own work.

Contents

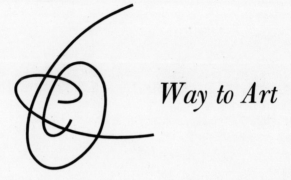

Way to Art

Scientific, Mystical, and Artistic Knowledge

Clearly, the invitation to find in art a key to the synthesis being sought by Western man requires a new approach. Because of the definitions given by theories and implied in much recent practice of art, this invitation seems to suggest that what I advocate is either hedonism or escapism. These are not my intentions.

Sir Arthur Eddington, in "The Nature of the Physical World," remarks that there exist two kinds of knowledge, which he calls symbolic and intimate. To illustrate, he describes a visitor to the beach who, interested in the actions of wind, water, and waves, consults the science of wave mechanics and finds in its mathematical laws the answer to his quest for symbolic knowledge. At another time the visitor remembers some lines of poetry and, contemplating the surf, gains some insight into nature which, though not described by physics, satisfies his quest for intimate knowledge. It is Eddington's belief that these two kinds of knowledge exist independently side by side in man's consciousness.

This dualistic concept of two independent kinds of knowledge has shaped Western man's attitude toward reality, particularly during the past hundred and fifty years. I do not think it greatly distorts Eddington's idea to identify his two ways of gaining knowledge as science and mysticism. Considering the preference Western civilization has given science as the more useful, trustworthy, and objective of the two, and the corresponding devaluation of mysticism to a mere source of private insights, it is not difficult to recognize Eddington's equal acceptance of the two as a step toward a possible union. The new synthesis requires the consummation of this union.

Either scientific or mystical knowledge appeals to only part of the whole man. Science appeals to the detached, analytical, disciplined, and objective mind that is not swayed by emotional reactions. Mysticism appeals to a desire for emotional involvement, to a sense of empathy negating the critical self. This is the Apollonian and Dionysian polarity of the Greek drama, superficially resolved by putting the two sides of man in two separate categories.

The whole man is not satisfied with this division. Modern science offers him proof that mystical knowledge contributes to scientific progress, as in the work of Einstein or Freud. Modern art shows him the contribution that scientific knowledge makes to the mystical insights of painting, as in the work of Mondrian or Cézanne. Modern man wonders whether the dualism of science and mysticism may not be transcended in the synthesis of an attitude toward reality including all his own faculties. I suggest that this synthesis is effected in works of art and that it becomes manifest through an attitude of participation.

The differences in the attitudes involved here may be illuminated by giving three different definitions of reality. For science, reality consists of facts; for mysticism, it dissolves into sensations; for the arts, it is a chain of events. For example, a player on a football team does not have the same attitude as the spectator in the bleachers, who enjoys an emotional identification with his "side," nor does he have the attitude of his coach, who, ideally as a detached observer, makes scientific plans of strategy. The player combines the two attitudes. He is connected with the game through study and observation, thereby gaining symbolic or scientific knowledge, and through emotions and actions, thereby gaining intimate or mystical knowledge. His attitude, in short, achieves integrated knowledge through participation. Thus he achieves the synthesis desired by the whole man.

A participatory attitude is not restricted to football players. All reality can be known entirely through participation (this, perhaps, is what we call experience), just as it can be known partly through analysis and also partly through enjoyment and suffering. Because words in this context are essentially symbols conveying only scientific knowledge, an experiment may best illustrate what participation means and how scientific and mystical knowledge together contribute to the unitary awareness of reality needed for the wholeness of life and for a full appreciation of art and its function.

Before continuing, however, I want to point out that the polarity of science and mysticism employed here as a means to introduce the integration through art has been based on the popular concept of science as an accumulation of undisputed facts. With the similarly popular concept of art as a subjective expression of feeling, the polarity ought to have been shown as existing between science and art. Actually, recent developments in scientific thinking show—and I want to refer here to "Aspects of Form," a symposium edited by Lancelot Law Whyte, in which Herbert Read states that "Aesthetics is no longer an isolated science of beauty; science can no longer neglect aesthetic factors"—that creative science and creative art are in fact quite closely related. It is a shortcoming of terminology that makes it difficult to differentiate between science as a collection of facts and science as an expression of meaning; and art as the expression of meaning and art as the realization of private notions. I expect subsequent chapters to dispel these conceptual difficulties.

Ruesch and Bateson in "Communication" illustrate this unitary concept when they point out that man receives all information via nervous impulses that in effect do not differentiate between observational and empathic data.

Experiment in Participation

This experiment derives from acoustics, where certain facts can be expressed in simple, visual terms. A string of a musical instrument begins to vibrate when it has been plucked. These vibrations, simplified and exaggerated in profile, are represented in figure 1.

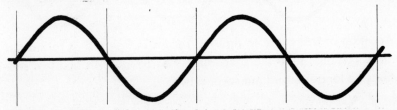

Figure 1

This is actually a vibration of pure pitch, which no instrument can produce. The timbre characterizing the instrument is the result of overtones sounding simultaneously on the same string. The curve of the octave above the keynote is shown in figure 2.

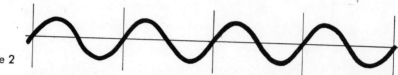

Figure 2

Combining these two curves as they are combined on the string, by adding their corresponding distances from the axis, produces figure 3.

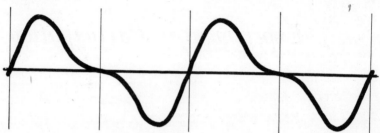

Figure 3

Another prominent overtone is the fifth, which produces three oscillations for every two of the keynote. Its profile is shown in figure 4.

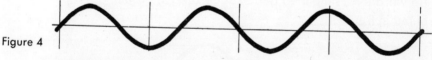

Figure 4

Addition of this curve to figure 3 results in figure 5, a formation more complex than the preceding ones because its first two sections no longer equal the second two.

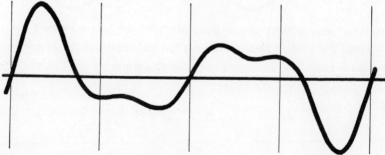

Figure 5

The four sections together repeat, however, as figure 6 reveals by showing a longer line.

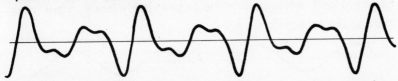

Figure 6

Adding oscillations from other instruments as they sound together in an orchestra results in sections of patterns as complex as the one represented in figure 7.

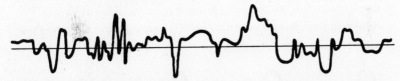

Figure 7

It can easily be observed that the tone of a piano key gradually dies down after being struck. Although the string continues to oscillate at the same frequency, the amplitude of its waves decreases. Figure 8 illustrates this process.

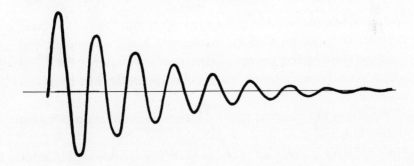

Figure 8

So far I have considered the wave image in terms of observation. Now, for actual participation, cover figure 9 with a piece of paper and, while pulling the paper slowly aside, focus attention on the emerging curve.

Figure 9

Thus you have become aware of a definite reaction. An initial feeling of expectation gives way, after a few ups and downs of the curve's movement, to a sensation of comfort (which will become stronger after repeating the experiment a few times).

Make the same test with figure 10, and you will find that these sensations are intensified.

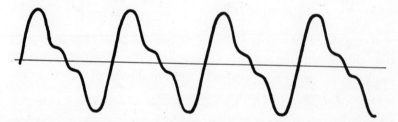

Figure 10

The movement demanded of the eye is more vigorous and induces a stronger reaction; also the movement is more complex and causes a more lasting interest. Yet here, as with figure 9, the initial alarm subsides as soon as the regular repetition has been discovered.

Watching the curve of figure 11 emerge produces a different state—insecurity.

The sudden and irregular changes seem unjustified; expectations are disappointed; the desire to understand has been thwarted.

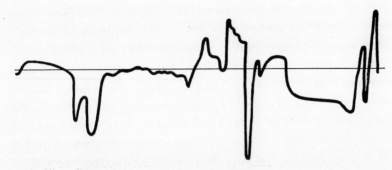

Figure 11

Various conclusions can be drawn from these experiments: In-harmonious and unpredictable challenges cause irritation, and rhythmic ones create pleasure eventually deteriorating into bore-dom. It is tempting to investigate the reasons for these reactions, but such investigation would lead to purely scientific procedures. The most important result of the experiments is the complex re-sponse, involving both body and mind, to a stimulus with a direct and immediate effect.

It is important to recognize this immediacy, for it is a touchstone of true participation. Traditionally, our tendency has been first to observe, then to understand, and only then to respond "emotion-ally." By this method—which, incidentally, we have been con-ditioned to recognize as the only civilized one—there is no re-sponse to the stimulus itself but only to what has been filtered from it by the mind. This indirect response has its advantages in that it avoids involvement, disappointment, and suffering—which is why it has been advocated. But by adopting this method of indirect reaction, although it increases our short-range security, society has reduced unitary man and, as will become apparent presently, has renounced the vital contribution of art.

In the experiments themselves, the initial scientific observations have offered no preparation for the participatory sensations. After having participated, a person should find those observations helpful in correlating isolated experiences and leading to further participation in rhythm in nature as well as in art. Observation thus used as a tool of participation helps to intensify the development toward unity. To participate fully in an event, in short, it is necessary to reverse the customary procedure and to allow the reaction first and then to clarify and expand the reaction through observation and analysis.

Way to Art

The readiness to participate opens a way to an understanding of reality more complete and profound than intellect or emotion alone can offer. This unitary attitude also opens the way to art. I intend to show later how throughout history vital art declines during periods of more analytical attitudes—as, for example, in the years between Pericles and Plato—and that the vitality of art is restored when unitary man reasserts himself—as he did at the end of the Dark Ages, for example, and as he is beginning to do today. Assuming for the moment a work of art to be only a harmonious piece of reality, its influence on the beholder may be described in terms of oscillations, relating the preceding wave experiments to art through a symbolic parallel.

The vaccillating upper curve of figure 12 represents the uncertainties of the beholder. Under the impact of the rhythmic order of a work of art, symbolically indicated in the second curve, the beholder's oscillations are transposed into a state of similar order. The lower curve shows this relative clarification. The margins paralleling the axes of oscillation illustrate thresholds of response. Any disturbance of equilibrium must reach a certain

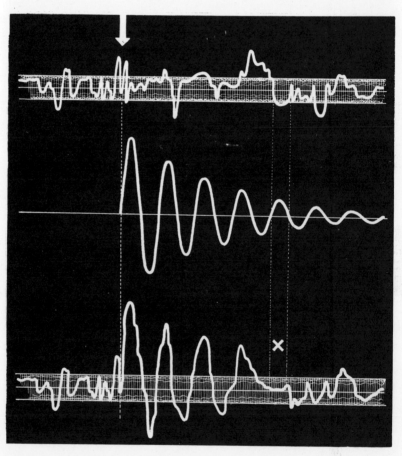

Figure 12

degree of intensity before it can be registered by the nervous system. The width of this margin indicates a person's sensibility. For a very insensitive observer this margin may be so wide as to envelop the whole event depicted, and he may then be unable to register the impact of many works of art.

At point X the phenomenon of interference is illustrated—a wave and a trough neutralize one another. The possibility of such neutralization indicates that if an observer is not attuned to a specific work of art, its effect upon him may be nil in spite of his sensitivity. At other times, under changed conditions, the same work of art may have on him a profound impact of lasting significance.

Figure 12 also indicates that the process of art involves time. The influence of a work of art has a beginning and an end. This is true for the individual event of experiencing a work of art: a person may understand and abandon it quickly, or he may be occupied with it for a long time. It is also true for the meaning of works of art for whole periods of civilization: a person may return again and again to certain masterpieces because he is aware of their actuality, or he may feel their significance fade. The Acropolis has always been a symbol of fine art; Shakespeare's message was lost on the people of the Enlightenment but was rediscovered by the Romantics. Bach's compositions meant dry exercises to such nineteenth-century Romantic composers as Tchaikovsky. Concert audiences today consider them sublime music. "Vita brevis, ars longa" is an old saying. But its truth should not prevent reliance on a personal response in every exposure to art; and a person should not feel slighted if, despite his efforts to listen and to understand, a work of art does not speak to him. It may do so at some other time; it may be speaking to others. A work of art may sleep, it may die, and it may suddenly return to life.

The appreciation of art, symbolically illustrated in figure 12, remains incomplete if it is understood only in the form of individual beholders participating in aesthetic values. This has been the custom for a long time, based again on the separation of science and art. To overcome this limitation and to recognize the integrating power of art, both the beholder and the work of art must be considered under broader aspects—not new perhaps, but long overlooked and uncovered only recently.

Psychoanalysis has shown that man is essentially not an independent rationalistic being, connected with his surroundings by observation, analysis, and action based on evaluation of facts. He is rather a vortex of energies interacting with other vortexes or organizations of energy with or without his knowledge and intention. Man's rational faculties appear to be organs of adjustment rather than of supreme control. Depth psychology also has shown that, although consciousness seems to single him out, man's subconscious qualities, energies, and drives are like roots of trees in a forest, intertwined with other roots and connecting with a common soil. Thus the whole man, like the football player, is part of a team, a member of a group or a community as much as he is an individual.

Similarly, a work of art is more than a beautiful piece of design fashioned by some aesthetically gifted individual. The artist, in E. M. Forster's phrase, "lets down as it were a bucket into his subconscious, and draws up something which is normally beyond his reach. He mixes this thing with his normal experiences, and out of this mixture he makes a work of art." This gift of shaping the formless content of this "bucket" by means of his "normal," or conscious, knowledge is the gift of creativity; it is the gift by which the artist speaks of and to his audience. What the artist consciously knows is his own individualized insight. What he does not know in this sense—the stuff from his subconscious—is what he shares with others; it is largely communal property. This common background determines what is called the philosophy of a time and place. It is compounded of traditions and hopes; it is the values by which a community lives—it is their way of life. This way of life is subtly and constantly changing; its values and behavior patterns are continuously in a state of adjustment, and its symbols never stop becoming obsolete. The artist, a person gifted with exceptional sensitivities and forming powers, creates new symbols expressing these inchoate values. Through his work he helps to clarify and establish the values that determine his fellow men's adjustment to new conditions of living.

From the idea of the whole man participating in social processes, the values of which the artist symbolically expresses and thus helps to consummate, emerges a new definition of art. Art is meaning expressed in a form commensurate with the whole man.

Understood in this inclusive sense, art is more than works of fine art. It becomes an ingredient of all we do and make, indispensable for a unitary life. Art pervades the simplest tool—which must be more than utilitarian to satisfy truly the whole man—as it pervades a painting that reflects the philosophy of its creator and, through him, of his time. Art is part of a building as it is part of a chair, of a good meal, or of human intercourse. And it is part of music, sculpture, and poetry.

With this all-pervasiveness, art, seen no longer separate from the events of living, again becomes a nucleus around which the new synthesis of a coherent pattern of meaning may crystallize. When we participate in art, we may thus receive enlightenment about questions that both the detached critic and the dissolved emotionalist can neither answer nor fully comprehend.

Portraits and Capitals

Art, as a concern of community revealed through participation, has dimensions that description alone cannot properly illuminate. An experience of art as the symbolic expression of a way of life may serve better to illustrate this concept. A series of portrait sculptures in juxtaposition with architectural capitals have been selected for the following reasons.

The capital has had an almost unchanged purpose throughout the history of Western art: its function has been that of a mediator between pillars or columns and their burden of lintels and arches. This continuity of function gives the capital an understandable symbolic value as the bearer of an architectural burden. That the capital was intended to be a symbol is suggested by the amount of creative effort lavished on this particular building element. The technological functions of a building do not require an elaborate capital; any square stone would have sufficed to accommodate the ends of lintels and the springers of arches.

The meaning embodied in the symbol of the capital may be described as offering an answer to the question of how to bear a burden—a question that has been asked by every generation since the beginning of time. For although this question has often been answered many times in the course of history—and although all these answers may have given the people of their time the common interpretation of their task, as it is the function of art to do—the conditions of life have been changing and its problems have not remained solved.

A way of life as a concept is an elusive thing. It is a complex composite more protean than the sea. There exists no visual symbol of a way of life in such a simplified form that it can be directly compared with a capital. Any verbal description, on the other hand, would involve a change of medium likely to obscure the experience that such comparison should induce.

The art of portrait sculpture here suggests that a way of life is recorded not only in the pages of history; a way of life also leaves its imprint on the people who have lived it. Fashions, traditions, habits, surroundings, ideals of the society in which he lives—all mold a man's features. Wherever a sculptor has preserved the forms of man's countenance in stone or bronze, he has created a condensed yet comprehensive record, not of the way of life itself perhaps, but of its specific forming powers. It would be hazardous to base any judgment of the qualities of a historical period on only the facial expression of one of its contemporaries. Yet it is surprising to discover how much the typical prevails in any group of portraits created in the same cultural orbit. The

typical is so prevalent, indeed, that the sensitive eye has no difficulties in placing any given portrait in its proper group, feeling
it to express the way of life of its time.

The following plates show sixteen capitals, selected from
various periods of Western heritage, in juxtaposition with portraits fashioned at the same time and place. They are matched so
closely that the portraitist may have met the sculptor who performed the architectural task. These illustrations are shown without legends to invite the participatory approach. They are
preceded, however, by a schematic presentation of their inter-
relations. This diagram shows the skeleton, or rather the river
system, around which Western civilization has grown. Dotted
lines indicate general, here undefined, influences, such as those
exercised through trade relations or vague memories; heavy solid
lines indicate direct heritage, such as those from parents to children; light solid lines indicate conscious, intentional return to
sources other than those of immediate descent. The open-ended
dotted lines at various points of the diagram indicate influences
from the East and from various so-called primitive cultures. Comparison of the illustrations along these lines, as well as in the
sequence in which they appear, will reveal the complexity of
Western tradition and will serve incidentally as an introduction
to the main part of this study. However, the primary purpose of
these illustrations is to show the feasibility of a participatory
approach to art.

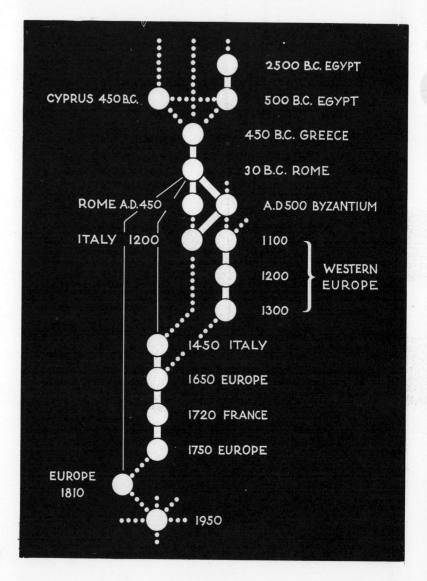

CYPRUS 450 B.C.

2500 B.C. EGYPT

500 B.C. EGYPT

450 B.C. GREECE

30 B.C. ROME

ROME A.D.450

A.D 500 BYZANTIUM

ITALY 1200

1100

1200 } WESTERN EUROPE

1300

1450 ITALY

1650 EUROPE

1720 FRANCE

1750 EUROPE

EUROPE 1810

1950

Figure 13

2500
BC

Figure 14

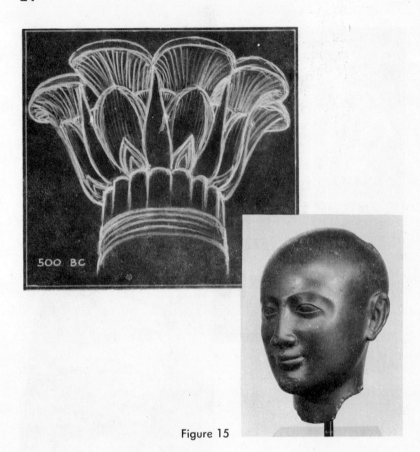

500 BC

Figure 15

450 BC

Figure 16

450 BC

Figure 17

30 BC

Figure 18

Figure 19

Figure 20

1100

Figure 21

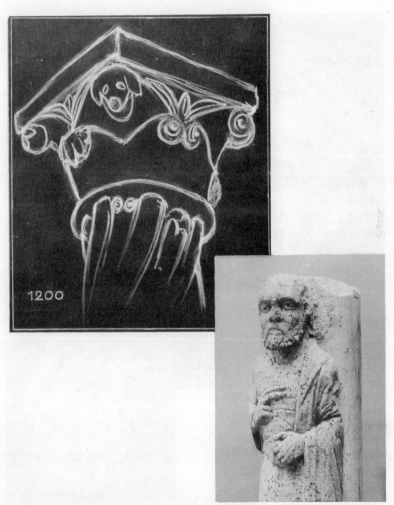

Figure 22

1200

Figure 23

Figure 24

1450

Figure 25

1650

Figure 26

1720

Figure 27

1750

Figure 28

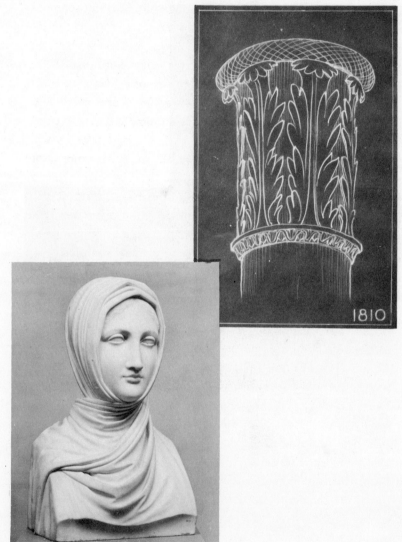

1810

Figure 29

If, then, in beholding these illustrations, the kinship between these portraits and these capitals is experienced, if there can be seen in the faces of these people the imprint of their way of life that challenged the sculptor to form this and no other capital, and if there can be felt the specific expressions of these capitals for their contemporaries—then the impression these heads and capitals convey will have provided a consummate experience of art. The person who examines these portraits and capitals will probably ask himself what particular shapes, proportions, or images are responsible for his reactions. Thus he will begin to analyze his impressions, thereby deepening his understanding. But if he fails to grasp the meaningful form of these images, then those analytical questions will fail to bring participation closer. Similarly, the beauty of many of these pieces of sculpture will impress the beholder. Yet when they are approached only for the purpose of yielding aesthetic pleasure, the profundity of their artistic meaning will remain undiscovered.

Figure 29 shows the influence of the neoclassic ideas that penetrated Western culture in the period of the French and American revolutions. This capital, as well as the two preceding it, were taken from furniture, because the architectural capitals of their time were no longer creative expressions but were resuscitations of classic forms.

Aside from isolated experiments without consequence, Western civilization has not created a capital since the years of the Baroque. This fact in itself, of course, is no sign of a lack of creativeness: the development of contemporary architecture shows that other symbols have come to be used as a means of artistic expression. However, it would have been revealing to extend the

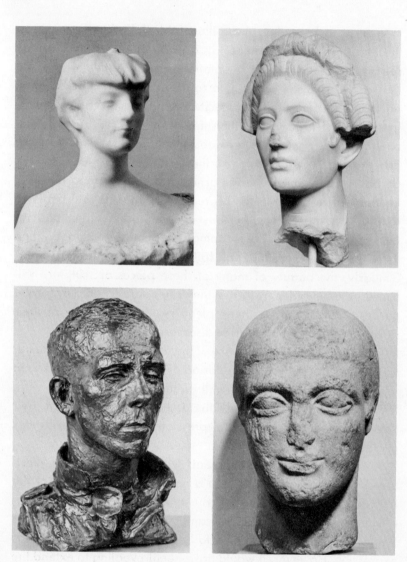

Figure 30

discussion here into the present day. The two portraits shown on the left side of figure 30 express attitudes toward life that seem familiar, attitudes encountered almost every day. Trying to visualize capitals corresponding to these expressions is to participate symbolically in the creative efforts of contemporary artists. The two portraits from ancient Rome and early Greece depict perhaps persons of comparable station in life, a lady and a soldier. It would not be difficult to derive from their features the elements of expression necessary for the designing of a fitting capital for them. The difficulties involved in doing the same for our contemporaries indicate the difficulties of creating and recognizing contemporary form. Finding this form is the task that we, together with contemporary artists, are obliged to solve.

Civilization and Form

Quest for Form

Western civilization is passing through a period in which man is rapidly abandoning concepts and forms that have outlived their usefulness; at the same time he is creating new ones that are more appropriate for his needs. Such a time of transition is also a time of uncertainty—an uncertainty that is felt today in many ways. Some persons feel aimlessly unhappy; others forget their doubts in work; still others, in pleasure. Those who have the courage to search for the meaning of their existence find no certainty within the confines of their private lives. They realize the old truth that meaning cannot be found within the individual; consequently they turn to the family and live for their children. Yet in this fulfillment of the desire for continuance they discover that, instead of finding the answer to the quest for meaning, they are postponing it. Thus man comes to expect assurance from groups larger than the family. He turns to friends, church, nation, community. He realizes that individuals do not exist by themselves; instead they form part of human society and need to participate in it. On the basis of this relation, man expects society to offer him a framework of meaning, a set of values against which he can check and adjust his individual judgment of good and bad, of right and wrong, artistic and inartistic.

In other words, the values by which man determines the quality and meaning of his existence are only in part of his own making. He must receive the directives for his evaluations from the social body of which he is a member. If these values are well established socially, they form the framework within which the individual finds his security and happiness. If they are doubtful or nonexistent, the individual finds himself confronted with more problems than he can solve. It thus appears that, from the point of view of the individual, the establishment of values is the main function of society; values form its tissue and ligament, if not its very substance. This framework of values constitutes what I have called the form of society.

In large areas of social existence today this form seems solid enough for us to rely upon it without question. It is implied in the pattern of social intercourse. It appears in the dictates of fashion. No woman, despite her wish to dress according to her personality, would dream of wearing the clothes that would have been fashionable at the time of her mother's wedding; she willingly subordinates her wishes to social form currently in vogue. Social form is also accepted in the institution and rites of marriage and, usually, in government and law.

However, beyond these established norms uncertainty mounts and standards of judgment become less objective. To take an example from our immediate surroundings, tools for living, china, chairs, houses, and cities show few qualities that seem generally acceptable. It may be argued that it is quite in the nature of things that objects made for private use are no concern of society; but the anxiety to "buy the right things" shows that there is more involved here than personal taste. Houses, moreover, exist not only in the private sphere of the owner but also in the spheres of the neighbor and the passer-by, who see them from the street. Houses and streets together form a town, in which there is an example of the pernicious results of weakened social form. For the past three generations towns and cities—the visible form of community—have been deteriorating. The town, from being the pleasant shelter comparable with a larger home it was in earlier days, has become a congested heap of stones, full of noise, dirt, and slums inimical to life. It has become a place from which those who can afford it move away into garden cities and restricted areas in the outskirts. The gist of all the arguments on this issue of city deterioration is that the average citizen no longer feels the community spirit necessary for the harmonious functioning of the body politic, and that consequently he has no interest in establishing or maintaining an outer form for his community commensurate with such harmony. This argument reveals that social form in the realm of communal existence is not strong enough today to coördinate man's various needs of shelter and traffic into a consistent pattern of urban development.

However, in spite of such disturbing developments, our cities still show a modicum of form. The citizens in their daily pursuits become aware of acute threats to the functioning of their community—for instance, traffic hazards—and insist that their city council take countermeasures to maintain these functions. This same element of emergency measures, precarious as it is, seems to be all that maintains the functioning of larger political bodies and international organizations. Undoubtedly a more reliable form, presumably expressed in long-range programs, would offer the citizens greater direction and security than the policy of meeting emergencies on a short-term basis. This lack of program betrays the weakness in the framework of social form.

A closer scrutiny of this weakness of social form on the political level reveals that it is only a symptom of a lack of form in the more fundamental issues of thought and feeling. Here there are philosophies and ideas of quite incompatible character existing side by side. Of such basic concepts of freedom, equality, authority, to name only a few, we possess no generally accepted interpretation; and the various existing definitions of these and other concepts support the most divergent political, economical, and educational schemes.

Underlying these philosophies and ideas are man's elemental drives, his emotions, his hopes, and his fears. In this region social form is lacking to such an extent that man is reduced to live almost completely in his private world, without adequate means of communication and thus without objective orientation, resulting in the present-day weakness of social form. The isolation it produces threatens man's mental health, as psychiatrists emphasize. In his emotional isolation man is unable to infuse this form with the vitality that should arise from unitary life.

The traditional vehicles for communicating unitary experiences have been the arts. A comparison of an objective language of form in art with the language of words, which is understood by most people, would indicate the existence of social form in emotional depths as well as on the rational surface. Today we own no such common language of art, although its groundwork, as I shall show, is being laid. Instead there are the small groups of artists and connoisseurs who may understand each other, but do not understand anyone outside their group, and who cannot be understood by outsiders. Art as a whole is still rather incoherent, which betrays the incoherence of form in the basic issues of social existence.

Man cannot live for long in such a state of uncertainty without sinking from the heights of human achievement and relapsing into states of barbarism. In recent history there have been disturbing evidences of this truth. Man's desire to push forward toward higher achievements prompts him to establish broadly reliable form. The present generation has made much progress toward accomplishing this form by recognizing the need for it and vigorously experimenting with a variety of answers.

How does man create this new form? I have shown that form cannot be established by deliberation only. Deliberation presupposes the unity of man's faculties—something he is still striving to achieve. Unitary man, in turn, cannot be satisfied with form only as a theoretical possibility; to him form must be a reality, accessible to his senses as well as to his mind. Such reality results from a unitary act, of which thought is but one facet. Form, therefore, must spring from what man is, from the experience that has formed him. It is from this unity that man understands the significance of cities, tools, and gestures as facets of social form, and appreciates the potency of art as the symbolic realization of such form.

Unitary man does not live only in the present moment. He has a sense of historic continuity and knows himself to be a link in the chain of tradition. As he elaborates the new form, it will be natural for him to look into history and see how other generations have coped with a similar problem. In the monuments of past periods of civilization he will find suggestions of what form once was and what it must become again. A survey of expressions of form in historical works of art will offer him a yardstick with which to measure his own efforts and achievements as he establishes the new form.

The art and form discussed in the following chapters represent history in terms of the family tree of Western civilization. One reason for this choice has been that our museums, schools, and publications offer very much more material on Western art than on any other art—material that offers readily available references for the following discussion. The other reason lies in the assumption that the traditions of a man's family offer better explanations for his inner problems than do the traditions of strangers. It is possible, of course, that the contrary assumption will prove to be true, and that comparisons with the arts and values of distinctly foreign civilizations—Oriental, African, or primitive—will be needed to make us aware of new possibilities for our own future. This would be the case if Western civilization should prove to have exhausted the available variations or capacities of its inherited patterns for living. The question cannot be decided before these patterns have been examined and their possibilities tested.

Space

Visiting historic monuments of art, in the hope of finding evidence of the inclusive form that, as I believe, must have existed during many periods of Western history, will demonstrate that these historic forms do not reveal their meaning as readily as might be hoped. Of the political systems of the past, of the philosophy and poetry that have been preserved through the centuries, of ancient paintings and sculptures, or of places where civilization once flourished—Egypt, Greece, Italy, or France—all that remains is parts and pieces, remnants without context. There are only tones without their chords, chords without their melodies: the symphony to which they belong—the whole that explains the parts—seems lost.

Faced with the difficulty of recapturing the unity of historic form from scattered fragments, we have often resigned ourselves to studying analytically the parts, hoping sometimes to grasp the meaning of their individual imagery. This approach has generally, for obvious reasons, not led to unitary synthesis. It implies so much conjecture that it inhibits the meaning of the form that has been partly recovered. Also the pattern of interpretation into which he fits these pieces of evidence is almost inescapably the beholder's own; it is hardly the one in which they originally functioned. Thus, it has been said that Egyptian painting is defective because it has no depth; Gothic tapestry, because it has no perspective; the Baroque church, because it shows no "befitting disdain for the flesh." If the achievements of the past were intended to satisfy present-day needs of form, then such judgments might be justified. If, however, historic form is studied for the purpose of clarifying contemporary form, then a more unitary method of interpretation must be found. Since the analytical technique is a typical instrument of modern rationalism, then it may be wondered whether this approach can resurrect the meaning of a historic form that probably was not governed exclusively by rationality. To avoid the pitfalls of analytic deductions, we need a clue that divulges the unity of the original pattern into which the remnants of historic form have been woven. It has always been hazardous to distill meaning from a single observation the relations of which are not known. It would be better to start from a framework revealing the structure and the proportions of the whole; then the meaning of the parts and pieces might be more easily understood.

I suggest that such a framework of historic form exists in the concepts of space that governed the imagination of our ancestors. Concepts of space are inclusive. If a person could grasp the specific significance of space for various periods of civilization, he might hope to find access to the meaning of their form as conveyed by their works of art.

At first, it will seem that space must always have presented an impalpable, limitless expanse in all directions. Indeed, from the sky-dome that capped the earth-disk of the Greeks to the four-dimensional continuum of relativity, space appears so endless in relation to the limited range of human activity that it seems unfit as a determinant of form. Yet man—not man the rationalist, but unitary man—rarely accepted the nihilistic endlessness of these spaces. He has always tried to interpret them, to relate them to his way of life. These very interpretive concepts of space have helped determine his realizations of form.

A simple example will illustrate these relations between space and form. Many museum visitors have been disturbed by the strange incomprehensibility, by the rigidity and deficiency, as they may have called it, of Egyptian sculptures. Indeed, these images of gods and kings may seem inane when seen against the neoclassic walls of exhibition galleries. Yet, considering the geography of Egypt—the long valley of the Nile cut into the lifeless expanse of barren desert, the arid rocks that are always in sight forbidding the very idea of moving away from the south-north flow of the life-giving stream—it may then be apparent that these Egyptian sculptures correspond with a concept of space quite different from our own. Today we can travel north and south, east and west with equal ease; going west in Egypt meant joining the dead behind the mountains at the setting sun. With such an insight into the specific quality of Egyptian space, the contemplator of Egyptian sculpture will correct his impression of spatial deficiency and will learn to interpret it as determined direction.

The following illustrations interpret some of the space concepts of Western history. They are drawings—not photographs—for several reasons. An illustration of space can be derived only from some spatial realization, since a concept of space as such is not visible. The spatial realizations of the past, however, are in most cases so incomplete, so damaged or spoiled by later changes, that their effect, when presented in photographs, becomes illusory. In a drawing, completeness can be achieved by integrating several pieces of reality found in different places; distracting details can also be suppressed, and an illusionistic art imbued with vividness. Furthermore, it is necessary to control the distortions that are unavoidable when a three-dimensional object is transposed into the two-dimensional flatness of a picture. In this case, where it is not objects but various kinds of spaces that a viewer wants to see, the mechanical perspective of the photographic lens, adapted to portray only one specific kind of space, cannot compete with the shifting human eye and the graphic record of its impressions.

I have illustrated the space concepts mainly by means of architectural elements, because walls form the most obvious definitions of space. In this context these elements are incidental only to the space they are meant to describe and not intrinsically relevant to its presentation. I might possibly have achieved a purer image of these spaces with arrangements of abstract planes. But the appreciation of such presentation would presuppose an eye trained by contemporary abstract painting—a presupposition unnecessary at this stage. The viewer is invited, therefore, to focus his attention on the space concepts these walls imply and to postpone the consideration of architecture. The text accompanying these drawings contains illustrations taken from existing records of the periods in question. They may serve to substantiate the impressions that the illusionistic presentations of space attempt to convey.

Photography is generally accepted today as the most "objective" method of recording reality, yet it is not universally useful. The problem of illustrating space will be considered later in connection with the art of painting. I shall show there that only Renaissance space can be illustrated adequately by the photographic camera—the camera being actually an application of research in the mechanics of perspective seeing, as carried out by Leonardo da Vinci, Dürer, and other artists at various times. Theirs was a space suited particularly for observation. It is revealing that we call the photographic record of the camera objective: its characteristic peephole quality isolates the beholder and restricts his immediate subjective participation. Other space records require participation rather than observation to reveal their meaning. Here the camera will not suffice. Participation in space, as a walk through the countryside shows, involves us more directly than does a look through a peephole. It is an experience that no picture can fully encompass. Even stereoscopic presentation, although more effective, will not cause the necessary involvement. A drawing promises to be more immediate in its effect. Because it leaves much to the imagination, it offers the best substitute for space itself—which a book cannot reproduce.

The space concept of Egypt, with its determined emphasis on the longitudinal component of space, fairly blocks the thought of developing in any other direction. Every movement here seems focused by some powerful agent on the road ahead.

Figure 1

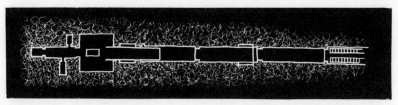

Figure 2

Figure 2, the plan of a tomb in the Valley of the Kings near Luxor, illustrates a realization of this almost one-dimensional concept.

This idea of space—to mention one of the implications of this approach to form—intimates that the paintings on Egyptian walls were not designed to confront the beholder as later paintings do. They seem rather intended to accompany him on his way. They appear to share his direction; they want to be noticed in passing, as it were, from the corner of the eye. When they are transplanted into foreign space—when they hang framed from modern walls—these paintings lose the meaning they are intended to convey. Figure 3, when seen at an angle rather than straight on, illustrates this possibility.

Figure 3

Figure 4

Figure 4 shows the temple district of Delphi in classic Greece and illustrates a lack of recognition of spatial order. Accomplished creations of sculpture and monumental architecture meet the eye in every direction; yet these creations do not stand in any discernible relation to each other. The spatial relations in which objects are placed, however, are the indicators of a spatial concept. There is the possibility that the Greeks, despite their accomplishments in sculpture, philosophy, and the arts of living, did not develop a spatial concept of consequence. Figure 5, a bird's eye view of the district, reveals this lack of interest in spatial relations.

Figure 5

Figure 6

This peculiarity of Greek culture will be evaluated later. Additional demonstration of this aspatial attitude may be found in the shift of emphasis in the Greek temple from the interior to the exterior, indicating a shift from spatial to sculptural architecture, and also in the chaotic political history of Greek cities, which never achieved the space-related concept of a nation.

The Romans, though in most respects heirs to Greek accomplishments, began to develop a space concept of their own. The Roman concept is not revealed so much in the representative public structures, which appear to have been rather intellectual and self-conscious attempts at monumentality, as in the more naïve development of their living quarters. Figure 7, taken from a wall painting in Herculaneum, exemplifies this Roman concept and reveals an attempt to organize space in its horizontal—that is, terrestrial—dimensions.

Figure 7

The Byzantines achieved the fusion of the materialism of Rome with the spirituality of the early Christians. By integrating the Roman accomplishment of organizing this world with the Christian accomplishment of organizing the hereafter, the Byzantines arrived at a concept of space as all-embracing as an eggshell.

Figure 8

It left no question unanswered, no desire unstilled. In fact, their definition of space quickly became so complete that it turned static, halting the quest for infinity and the desire for development, thus symbolizing the fate of Byzantine form—it could proceed only toward desiccation and petrification.

With the decline of Rome, a new vortex of cultural energy developed in northwestern Europe. Monks and knights labored and battled to weather the perils of chaotic centuries. They tried to save the values of Rome and of Christianity for a dream of unity, which was to come true later in the form of the Holy Roman Empire—an ideal of long persistence. Yet these values changed through the very efforts of preservation. With wilderness and danger at the door, and with the Unbelievers in the Holy Land, the contemplative life of the monks became charged with a fighting spirit, and many lords and barons expanded their concern for the family's domain into political and military action on a national scale. As soon as conditions permitted, the pent-up energies of cloisters and castles burst forth in a heroic attempt to establish the Kingdom of God on earth.

This audacious assault of the Romanesque gained its impetus with a conception of space that reached from the nether regions to the throne of God. The Romanesque space may be likened to a pyramid of dynamism, gathering energies at the base to thrust them upward toward heaven. Figure 10 reveals the energy of the Romanesque space in the underground crypt of the French church of St. Honorat.

Figure 9

Figure 10

In the concluding period of the Middle Ages—the Gothic—the aggressive energies of the Romanesque crusaders seem spent. The worship of Christ as the heavenly fighter has changed to prayers to the Virgin Mary asking for intercession and mercy. The efforts to establish the Kingdom of God on earth have given way to preparations for the hereafter. Life on earth has become focused on the day of judgment. Thus the Gothic concept of space has shrunk in its terrestrial dimensions and gathered its strength in the vertical, as a candle burning in the desire for redemption.

Figure 11

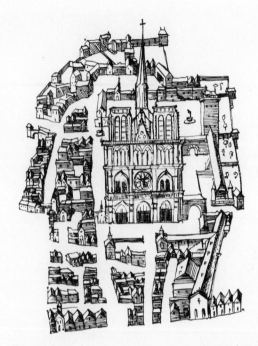

Figure 12

Figure 12, a section of a city plan of Paris from the end of the Middle Ages, illustrates the verticality of Gothic space.

Life on earth, however, went on, and new hopes were born that arrested the flight of the Gothic. Modern man made his appearance, trusting that with his newly sharpened tools of reason he might be able to meet all the problems that life imposed upon him. The people of the Italian Renaissance evolved a concept of space that was intelligently organized in accordance with the rules of rationality. This space permits mathematical Euclidean calculations. Figure 14, an ideal town plan suggested by Fra Giocondo, illuminates the aspirations of the Renaissance space.

Figure 13

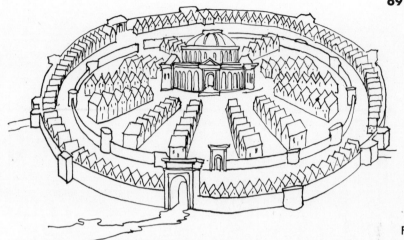

Figure 14

This sketch reveals a designer's attitude that today would popularly be called "scientific." Taking into account the changes in the economic structure of communities, Fra Giocondo's idea forecasts the geometric solutions to civic problems proposed by planning engineers today. The sketch also illuminates the static quality of Renaissance space: the town is envisioned as a completed monument and does not allow for growth. Partial execution as well as expansion would destroy the harmony of its proportions. Any change would ruin it.

The French ruling class of the sixteenth century, intrigued by the possibility of mastering reality through organization, went further. The almost mechanical accuracy of the space conception, with its strict construction around principles of axis and symmetry, tends to relegate any desire of spontaneous action or natural behavior to the level of indecency. The design for a park, shown in figure 16, may symbolize the idea of a conception that makes reason and law the essence of space.

Figure 15

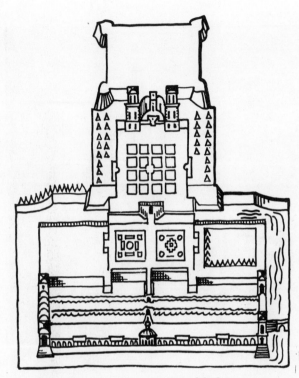

Figure 16

The Renaissance concept of space seems to have sufficed for only a rather short period. Its strict rationality was unable to accommodate man's emotional needs. To relieve this suppression, the Renaissance idea of space had to be amended. The people of the Baroque, schooled in self-consciousness by their Renaissance fathers, recognized the need for both intellectual clarity and emotional satisfaction. They elaborated a conception of space, combining static Renaissance clarity, centered on the beholder, with the dynamism of unfolding and becoming. Fontana's plan for the remodeling of the approaches to St. Peter's in Rome,

Figure 17

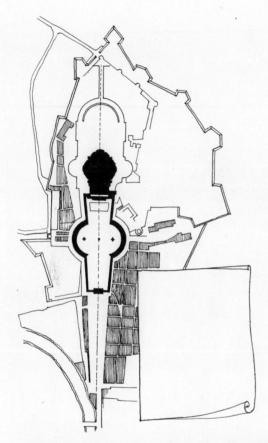

Figure 18

shown in Figure 18, emphasizes the combination of awareness
and enjoyment and reveals the ability of the connoisseur to relish
sophisticated arrangements of space. Some of this sophistication
has survived in the craft of stage designers whose theatrical settings we enjoy to this day.

In spite of such accomplishments as Fontana's, the attempt of
the early Baroque to balance rational and emotional elements

Figure 19

in its concept of space fell short of its goal. Cool calculation may still have been too strong, long-suppressed emotions still too aggressive to unite with accomplished grace.

It was only at the beginning of the eighteenth century that this balance came close to realization. Figure 19 illustrates this late-Baroque concept of space. This concept was to be maintained only for a short time; in that era they must have been conscious of the running sand in the hourglass. With great concentration, and sometimes with haste, they made use of their chance to mold lucidity, knowledge, fear, piety, and love into one flawless and enchanting unit—and they were conscious of what they were achieving. Perhaps in this consciousness, in this reflection, they found the gratification of their endeavors. The space concept of this period resembles, as Egon Friedell has suggested, a vast mirror, designed to focus upon the beholder every movement, every gesture, and every effect in constant reverberation. After the often turgid mixture of observation and sensation in the early Baroque, this later period rediscovered the possibility of unitary participation.

The plan of the Basilica of the Fourteen Saints in Upper Bavaria (fig. 20) reveals the mirrorlike reflectivity and unity of this spatial concept. A comparison with the plan of a Romanesque church intimates that, whereas the monks of that period were content with their self-effacement, the people of the late Baroque craved the consciousness of their piety. Without this consciousness, worship did not have the proper significance for them. The pilaster head of figure 21 suggests the delusive reality of an object caught between opposing mirrors: spatial echoes multiply its existence. The same reflection, leading as with spiral movements to height-

Figure 20

ened awareness, prevails in the music of the late Baroque—the time of Bach.

As the conception of Baroque space faded, Western civilization entered a period of fundamental changes. The French Revolution dissolved an age-old system of social orientation; scientific discoveries and technological advances expanded the dimensions of human potentialities; the United States won its independence

Figure 21

and opened new vistas to those whom Europe had disappointed. Artistically, too, man entered uncharted territory. Romantic music rebelled against the strictures of true classic form, and for the first time made an appeal to the untutored emotional nature of man. Poetry attempted to cope with the vastness of potential conceptions; painting invented new images to convey the new experience.

Somewhere in the development of the nineteenth century, however, a certain disappointment became apparent. Did changes come too fast for man to comprehend, or did man himself change too quickly to maintain the inner continuity of his growth? Whatever the cause, the result, as it appears today, was that man despaired of grasping the oneness of his new world—he failed to develop a comprehensive spatial concept. This failure found a symbolic expression in the new attitude of artists. They became content with incomplete aims and achievements. They grew experimental, tested devices or effects, sketched interesting details, or recorded observations. Those who still felt a need for unity retired into a private world of their own. Also the people at large, engaged in occupations growing increasingly specialized and unrelated on the level of individual experience, were deprived of any unifying interpretation that a common concept of space would have provided.

To compensate for this nonexistent conception of space, man had recourse to his latest achievement, the mechanical sciences. By suppressing the emotional part of his existence, he became able to accommodate himself to the inorganic, but logically valid directives of science. The mechanical gridiron plan of contemporary cities may serve as a symbol of the substitute that mechanical directives provided. This purely intellectual conception of space did not attempt to satisfy the requirements of unitary man. But man's emotional faculties had already atrophied through lack of stimulation. They no longer demanded their share of satisfaction in the brave new world; they even ceased to object to malignant formations.

Figure 22

Figure 22, a conglomeration of incompatible elements on Michigan Avenue in Chicago, illustrates a situation that under any unitary conception of space would have demanded immediate correction—if it could ever have developed.

During the first decades of the twentieth century, a new concept of space has begun to emerge, as well as a new pattern of living. In science, in medicine, in education, there are encouraging signs of the recognition that technology is not a cure-all but a tool the benefits of which depends on the wisdom with which man uses it. Instead of adjusting our existence to the exigencies of mechanization, we are beginning again to maintain the pri-

Figure 23

Figure 24

macy of unitary life. This unitary concept of life is still in a state of gestation, and so is the new concept of space. Developments in city planning, in painting, sculpture, and architecture suggest that man will integrate his dynamic interpretation of distance, time, and matter with the spiritual dimensions of unitary man.

The housing project in figure 24 illustrates the penetration of unitary considerations into the gridiron city plan. Figure 25, a clover-leaf intersection in the highway system of New York, illuminates the scope of the new vision. Here can be felt the breath of bold and courageous undertaking. Here can be sensed the beginning of the unitary order that man intends to impose upon the chaos bequeathed us by the nineteenth century.

The new concept of space promises eventually to embrace again man's vision of unity; it will also be flexible enough to accommodate individuality. Combining these two aspects of space, the new concept will dynamically transcend the static limitations observed in most space concepts of history. It will contribute toward a creation of form in modern society which will restore respect for the potentialities of the whole man.

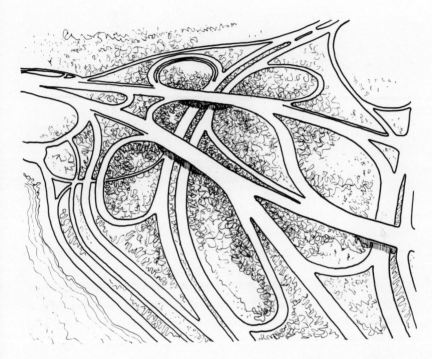

Figure 25

Sculpture

For the spectator who is familiar with the various concepts of space, sculpture is the most readily understood representative of historic form. Its subject matter is man—a familiar image and one most readily appreciated. The shapes of sculpture are real in the sense of three-dimensional spatial existence: they realize most clearly, therefore, the space concepts of their time. A sculptor transforms the shapes of the human body according to the idea of space governing the period in which he lives, thus illuminating the form of his time.

Any discussion of a unitary phenomenon, such as a work of art, involves a breakdown into component parts. Thus, a piece of sculpture can raise the two questions of what the sculptor says and of how he says it; or in other words, a basic approach to understanding can begin by differentiating between subject matter and form. Subject matter will be discussed below in conjunction with painting. Independent of whether the sculpture represents the human body or any other subject, sculptural form has two distinct aspects: sculptured shapes relate to the surrounding space; sculptured surfaces relate to the enclosed mass.

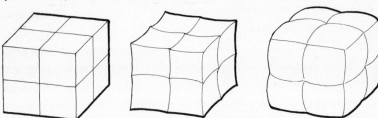

Figure 26

Consider first the surface-mass relationships. The stone, bronze, or clay of a sculpture is not an inert mass that simply ends at the surface; nor does it simply emulate the naturalistic outlines of the human body. Instead, sculptural surface seems to result from the struggle between a volume that tries to expand, as it were, and a skin that tries to hold it together. The three cubes in figure 26 typify this conflict between distention and restraint. The surfaces of the first cube are of no interest sculpturally. They are plane surfaces of lifeless rigidity. In its mechanical correctness, this cube arouses no interest concerning its substance, whether it is full or empty. The surfaces of the second cube, by contrast, are of sculptural significance. They seem tired and weak; they seem to enclose a passive content incapable of resistance. The third cube seems filled with energy; its content seems ready to burst forth, and the surfaces are taut in the effort to hold it together.

In any sculpture, the conflicting forces of distention and restraint are in a state of balance. There are different ways of

achieving this balance, and every period of civilization has suggested its own solution. These solutions are part of the form that
sculptors have endeavored to express. The actuality of this problem of balance accounts, to a large extent, for our interest in
sculpture today. The following plates illustrate some of the ways
of balancing inner and outer forces used by sculptors in the course
of Western civilization.

Figure 27 depicts the foot of an Egyptian statue. A powerful
surface here exercises rigid control over the plastic volume. Yet
this rigidity fully controls only the sides and the back of this shape;
the front suggests the possibility of a more liberal development.
This freedom in one direction relates this sculpture to the one-
dimensional space concept of Egypt. It also illuminates some
aspects of form in Egyptian civilization, notably the one-
dimensional continuum of ancestor worship.

Figure 28 pictures the knee of a youth carved in archaic
Greece. Although it is anatomically incorrect—or perhaps because of this fact—it reveals the restrictive force of a controlling
surface, suggesting a similarity with Egyptian sculpture. Yet there
is a decisive difference: the inner forces of the Greek sculpture
are not compelled to act in one direction only; they seem to apply
their pressure on all sides. Also, the skin imposes no restrictions
of prohibitive rigidity: it allows within its laws an all-around freedom. It is this balance of freedom and restraint that challenges
our imagination, and that has made Greek culture a source of
inspiration for Western man.

A few centuries later, the perfection of the archaic balance
begins to be disturbed. Figure 29 shows part of a body from the
altar of Pergamon, with an overstrained and tired surface barely

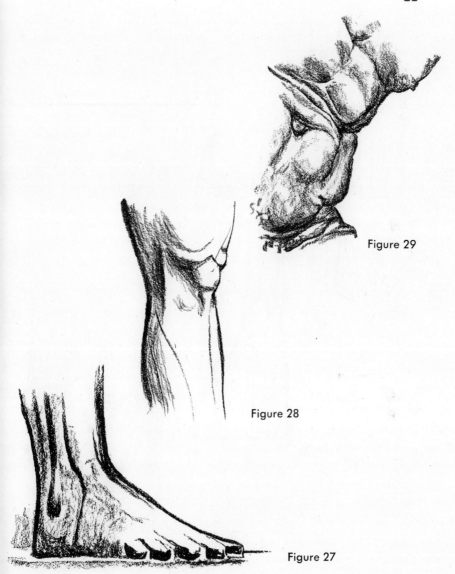

Figure 29

Figure 28

Figure 27

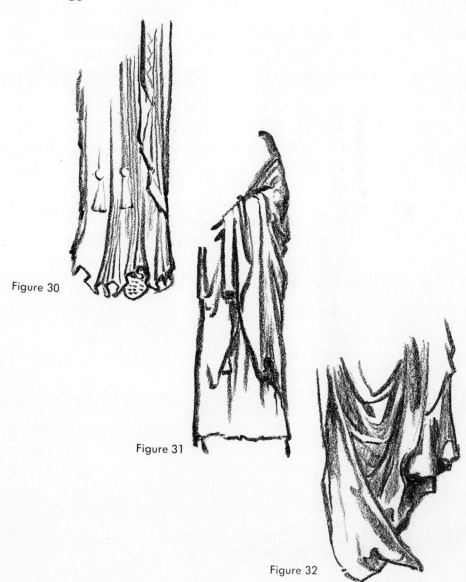

Figure 30

Figure 31

Figure 32

able to keep the seething masses together. Here the ordering forces have weakened and the anarchic forces have gained predominance. Indeed, this was the case not only in the artistic, but also in the social, history of Greece.

There is a similar progression from mastery of ordering surfaces to independence of anarchic inner forces in the development of the Gothic figure. These figures are usually clothed, and the folds of their garments offer a more energetic illustration of the shifting balance of forces than the human anatomy and impose less restrictions on the sculptor's imagination.

Figure 30 shows a surface of compelling strength that definitely prohibits any major motion other than vertical. It is not surprising that this figure was sculptured in the years when the French were preoccupied with the construction of their great cathedrals. Figure 31 illustrates a transitional figure with a fairly neutral balance of perhaps weakened forces. Figure 32 shows a virulence of inner activities not properly directed by the ordering forces of the surface. When this statue was carved, the Gothic idea had begun to succumb to the rationalistic ideals of the Renaissance, which sculptors soon expressed in measured idealizations of realistic anatomy.

The beard of a Baroque saint in figure 33, growing from a rigid face like flames from a burning log, illustrates how far inner forces can be allowed to develop without entailing anarchy; if the ordering concept remains strong and certain enough, the result is still harmony and the impact upon the beholder is commensurate with the forces deployed.

Figure 34 depicts weakness rather than strength. This portrait mask from the end of the nineteenth century reveals a shrunken

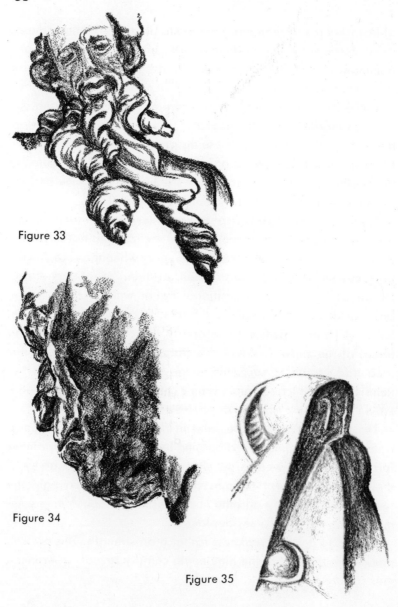

Figure 33

Figure 34

Figure 35

and brittle surface that seems unable to hold together any sculptural energies. Yet this weakened skin is not challenged by an inner desire for expansion. The mass of the sculpture seems just as weak as the surface. This common weakness explains the apparent balance—one without emphasis or challenge.

Figure 35 illustrates one aspect of contemporary sculpture. In times of emotional uncertainty, man is always tempted to rely on his rationality for the missing directive. This head of a hooded woman looking over her shoulder reveals the artistic weakness of such intellectual devices. The beholder would expect this head to express the inner strength or weakness of its semispherical shape in the development of the face. However, this is not carried through; instead, a mechanically plane surface prohibits its development. As a result the beholder is at a loss to know whether the shell is void of sculptural energy, or whether the expression of such energy has been stifled as if by an iron lid. The lack of emotional communication in this surface betrays its rationalistic origin.

A surface determined by a conflict of inner and outer forces is not the only means of sculptural definition. Especially in the period of predominantly cerebral approach to form through which we have been passing, rational indications of spatial limits, as unemotional as a sheet of glass, may suffice to define the shape of sculptured volumes. Yet unitary man is apparently not satisfied with this neglect of his sensory means of perception and emotional means of reaction. He expects not only to recognize but also to experience the conflict of the forces that determine the surface of sculpture—he wants to participate. The opposite extreme, the sensualism of dripping melted metal in some modern sculpture, will not meet this need.

Contemporary sculptors, with their problem clarified by the work of the constructivists, begin to respond to this need for unity. The revitalization of the sculptural surface can be most strikingly illustrated in contemporary pottery. Those who have attempted to use the potter's wheel will agree that the form-giving process involves sculptural surface in a very direct manner. The potter's fingers, controlled by his intentions as well as by the resistance of the material, strive to impose a form on the shapeless, but by no means impassive, lump of clay. The surface he achieves has a vibrant vitality because it results from the struggle between the inner, chaotic forces of the clay and the outer, ordering forces of the potter's hands. If the potter, however, is not engrossed in the process of his creation "with body and soul," if he has only a mental concept of form, then he will attempt to establish his shape with auxiliary, rationally contrived devices. The use of these more mechanically controlled tools does give precision to his work, but it also deadens the vitality of his surface. Moreover, these tools have to be applied to a clay that is hardened beyond the stage of plasticity. The structural quality the clay then displays resembles that of wood or leather; it invites the potter to create shapes that do not correspond with the fundamentally plastic character of his material. The misguided potter obliterates, together with a vivid surface, the suggestions of form that his material contributes to a vital work of art.

The profile of a pot offers a clear indication of the sculptural vitality of its creator and his time. Figure 36 illustrates two vessels from Greece: one from the beginning and the other from the end of the Greek creative classic period. The one at the left expresses in the vivacity of its profile the sureness and spontaneity of the

Figure 36

creative act that formed it. The one at the right illustrates how the refinements of an almost abstract form resulted in the eradication of all the surface qualities that would challenge the beholder's unitary response. What is left is the recognition of an allegedly Greek ideal of purity—an ideal that has been found to be largely the creation of eighteenth-century neoclassicists.

Figure 37 shows at the left a ceramic product of the late Italian Renaissance. This shape does not suggest clay as its material—instead it suggests metal. Furthermore, the inanity of its profile betrays a purely intellectual and eclectic conception of pottery.

The powerful profile of the pot at the right illustrates the revitalization of the sculptural concept characteristic of the present generation of potters. The form is not preconceived and mechan-

Figure 37

ically imposed; it results obviously from the struggle between the artist's will and his clay. The phases and the outcome of the struggle for form that the artist has expressed in the profile of his pot are the source of its impact upon the beholder. The clarity with which this pot shows the tension between mass and surface indicates that contemporary sculpture is rediscovering the meaning of this aspect of sculptural form.

The other major aspect of sculptural form, as I have suggested earlier, appears in the relation of the sculptured shapes to the surrounding space, as illustrated in figures 38–46. These figures indicate how closely the sculptor's interpretation of the human body relates to the space concept of his period. A comparison of these illustrations of sculpture with the corresponding ones on space shows an identity of expression that prevails in spite of the existing differences between the sculptural and the spatial medium. This identity reveals surely the influence of the form that governed society during the various periods of civilization.

Today, a new and dynamic conception of sculpture is in the process of development in conjunction with a dynamic concept of space. (It has found one expression, characteristically enough, in mobile sculptures which must be seen in motion to be fully understood.) Figure 47 illustrates the new approach to sculpture. This is a reproduction of a sculptor's drawing rather than an actual work of sculpture, because this drawing portrays vividly the dynamism of the new concept. The materialization of spatial tensions here attempted suggests what is probably the central problem of the new sculpture—the dynamic interpretation of spatial interdependence. The successful solution of this problem is likely to result in a framework cf form that is more adaptable and more inclusive than any Western man has ever used before.

The wealth of new materials and techniques still to be explored is one of the reasons why contemporary sculptors have not been more consistent in suggesting such form. Yet by recognizing this wealth they heighten the potentialities of the future. Sculptors today begin to appreciate the contributions that modern technology can make to our way of life. By admitting plastics, new metal alloys, and synthetic stonelike materials into the studio, in addition to the traditional marble, wood, and clay, the artists bridge the gap between art and engineering that has opened during the past hundred years and hindered the realization of many new and vital ideas. These are now beginning to develop—and they need only time to ripen.

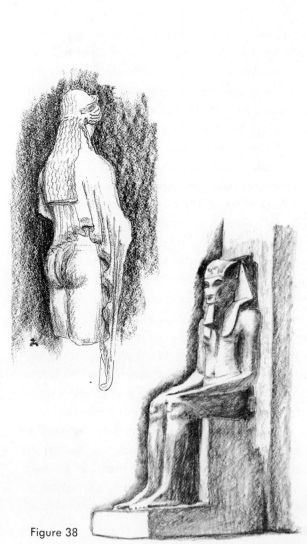

Figure 40

Figure 39

Figure 38

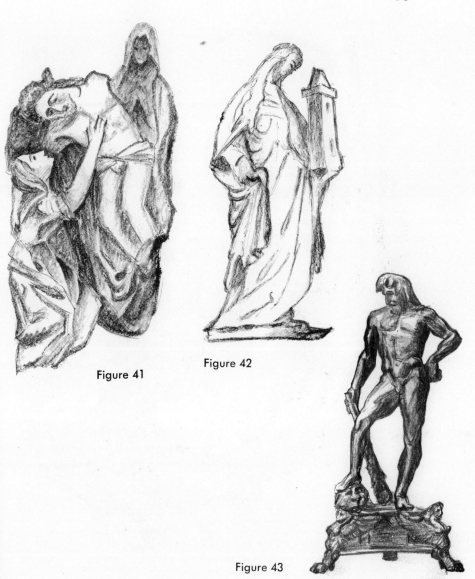

Figure 41

Figure 42

Figure 43

Figure 44

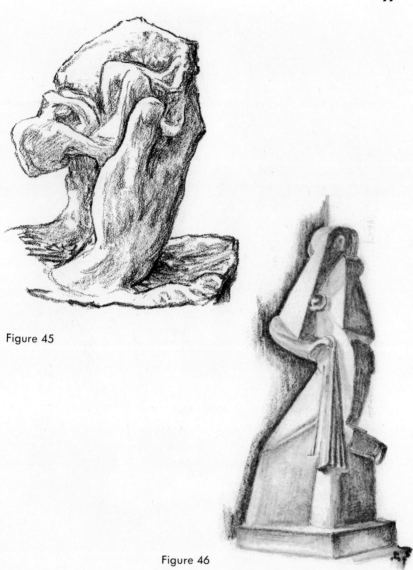

Figure 45

Figure 46

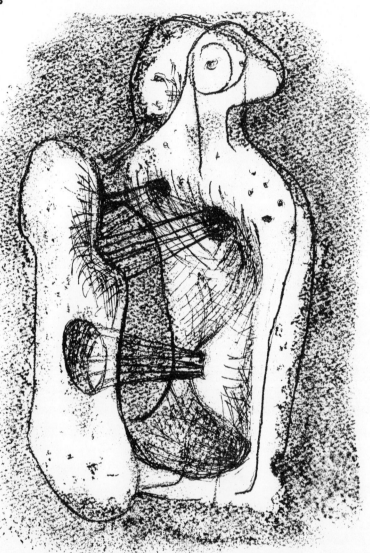

Figure 47

Tools for Living

Form, a function of the social group, is established with the assistance of the creative artist. Once defined, it controls the sculptor's concept of the human body. The illustrations of sculptures have indicated that the clarity of the sculptor's statement of the human body depends on the clarity and strength of the social form of his time. In periods of transition such as the present, the sculptor is forced to grope for a new definition of the space-volume relationships on which his work will be based. Under such circumstances the sculptor's efforts may come to resemble laboratory experiments that, as figure 47 has illustrated, are not easily understood by anyone who has not made it his special task to follow these experiments.

To illustrate the continuance of the historic problem of spatial form into the present day, it may be well, therefore, to consider

99

also the form of objects relating directly to practical, everyday needs. In these tools for living, practical functions take the place of the human body and act as the subject matter that has been shaped by the determinants of social form. If it were possible to choose for this inquiry a tool for living the function of which had not changed to the present day, the result would be additional insight into the form of the past as well as heightened appreciation of the form being created today.

Function in a tool for living involves both practical and human elements—a fact that friends of the slogan "Form follows function" have sometimes overlooked. Actually, the choice of tools for living with unchanged function as required here is limited because sometimes their practical, but more often their human, determinants are no longer evident. Many historic tools for living have been preserved, their function is often lost. Part of this function disappeared with those who used them; another part vanished when collectors and historians transposed certain objects into the fine arts, thus destroying the web of functional relations that gave these pieces their original significance. (A similar result has occurred when sculptures have been taken out of their spatial context.) Occasionally the functional significance of tools for living has been preserved, but then that function itself, while partly determining form, has been changed by changing formal factors. A period chair, for instance, expresses a way of sitting that cannot be fully appreciated without studying the costumes and social habits of its time, which differ considerably and often decisively from the costumes and habits of today. Only in very elemental tools are there functions that have not been seriously affected by changing habits.

The pouring vessel is such a tool. Its function is simple: it is a container to be lifted by a handle and tilted in such a way as to dispense its content through a spout or over a lip. Its meaning is determined by the way of life of the people who made and have used it. Its shape is the result of the integration of function and meaning, conditioned to some extent by the materials and techniques employed in making it. The drawings on the following pages show historical pouring vessels. They are arranged in chronological sequence and, like stepping stones, lead to the possibilities of contemporary form.

Viewing these vessels, the reader is again invited to exercise his imagination and to visualize these objects in their relations to the sculptures and spatial realizations shown in the preceding chapters. The civilization of the past few generations has been so largely imitative in the designs of tools for living that many of these vessels will seem to strike an oddly familiar note, having been seen—mainly as copies, no doubt—in settings that, for the purpose of this study, are quite out of context. They may evoke, therefore, personal reactions of like and dislike that are here beside the point. Also, museums and other collections have displayed such objects as these, inviting purely aesthetic responses to isolated works of art. Because it is not possible at this point to offer a reconstruction of the framework of cultural form sufficient to relate these vessels to their proper setting—it is the purpose of this study as a whole to accomplish this—the reader's imagination must assist in supplying the necessary visual continuity between concepts of space, sculptures, and such spatial objects as the pouring vessels shown on the following pages.

The Egyptian pitcher of figure 48 may serve to destroy any preconceived notion of the continuous progress of artistic achievement. The honesty with which use and technique have been combined here give this pitcher a nobleness of shape that has not been surpassed to this day.

The Iranian drinking bottle illustrates the influence of function upon shape. Intended to be lifted to the mouth so that the flow of wine can be caught with the lips, this bottle shows handle and spout joined together on one side of the narrow neck. The virile directness and the sincerity in the use of clay reflect the spirit of the people who created this vessel.

The Greek pitcher was made when archaic forming power had reached its peak. It reveals an attainment of balance between vigor and restraint that the Greeks themselves were unable to surpass. With the decline of their sculpture into naturalism, the noble shapes of their pottery began to wither and harden (see figure 36). The rigidity there no longer reveals the pleasures of creating and participating in living form.

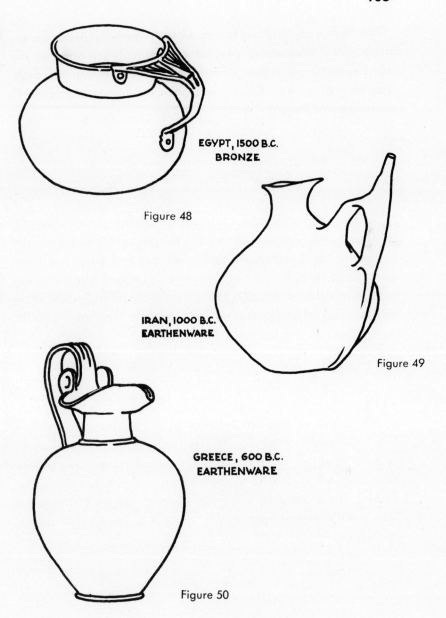

EGYPT, 1500 B.C.
BRONZE

Figure 48

IRAN, 1000 B.C.
EARTHENWARE

Figure 49

GREECE, 600 B.C.
EARTHENWARE

Figure 50

The Gothic jug strikes a balance between earthiness and aspiration. The unadorned display of its gray metal emphasizes the achievement of its maker in integrating the needs of the flesh, represented by the solid volume, with the needs of the spirit, symbolized in the pure, uplifting profile.

The Venetian vessel, by contrast, reveals the playful, literary, "nonfunctional" attitude of its time. In spite of the refinement of its general appearance, the various elements of this composition do not add up to a meaningful shape of unitary character. The spout, for instance, shaped like an animal's head, makes sense only through an implication not applicable to the foot or handle.

The teapot of colonial America again achieves integration. The importance of the family ties and neighborly relations of pioneering days, which found their symbol in mealtime gatherings, are well expressed in the interplay of pot, handle, spout, and lid. These powerful individual elements derive their strength from their interdependence; thus this pot is a symbol of unitary relations.

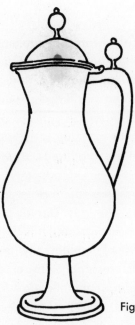

GOTHIC
GERMANY, 1350 A.D.
PEWTER

Figure 51

RENAISSANCE
VENICE, 1500 A.D.
ENAMEL

Figure 52

BAROQUE
BOSTON, 1710
SILVER

Figure 53

The two English teapots of black "basalt" ware offer telling illustrations of the petrifaction that befell the vigorous form of the Baroque in the period of the French Revolution. Neoclassic ideas of the "noble simplicity of Greece" prompted this development toward stern and austere shapes. The rigidity of this concept of form was necessary, perhaps, to assure and to guide a society threatened by the oncoming dissolution of the established pattern of living.

We know today that the neoclassic form was too "brittle" to withstand the shock of nineteenth-century changes. Unable to assimilate the riches that technology was bestowing, and afflicted with vertigo by the newly opened vistas, society temporarily lost all sense of proportion and form. Manufacturers, eager to serve an insatiable market, raided history, nature, and the arts in search for ideas, shapes, and décors. The freak house-shaped teapot of figure 56, probably intended as a joke when its original was made in 1750, is an example of what the Victorian era later produced in dead earnest.

These illustrations of pouring vessels show the ingenuity and vitality with which their makers combined practicality and significance in shapes of great beauty. The lack of ingenuity and vitality in most of the creations of the nineteenth century shows a serious neglect of human values during that era. This may indicate a lack of organic strength; society can hardly have a very healthy constitution if it allows meaningful form to deteriorate into meaningless imitation and inane decoration. The nineteenth century had enough reserve strength, however, for certain individuals to protest against such degradation. Ruskin, Thoreau, Morris, and Sullivan, among others, sought a nucleus of meaning around which a

Figure 54

**NEO-CLASSIC
WEDGWOOD, 1790
PORCELAIN**

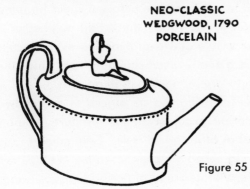

Figure 55

**ENGLAND, 1730
STONEWARE**

Figure 56

new form might crystallize. Ruskin and Morris made abortive attempts to revive medieval concepts of unity between culture and civilization. Henry Thoreau and Louis Sullivan—with a deeper insight and a greater optimism given them, perhaps, by the youthful energies of the New World—foresaw the growth of a new form out of the unitary coördination of the potentialities of modern man.

These prophets lived too early, however, to witness the new departure. The progress of technology, with all its economic and social implications, had to run its course before it could be fitted into a pattern of human living. Today the broad outlines of a changed world become visible and man experiences the inception of a new form. It is a Janus-faced situation from which the development of contemporary form takes its departure.

Most of today's tools for living can be placed in one of two groups. The first, or period group, contains furniture, houses, tableware, and accessories of historical styles. Continuing to use the symbol of the pouring vessel, I have chosen the Wedgwood pot of figure 57 to represent this group of period tools for living. This pot was made only a few years ago after an eighteenth-century pattern. These tools for living—some of them genuine, most of them "period-styled" or imitated—are valued and used today because they are felt to express certain habits of gracious living that are not incorporated in the products of the nineteenth and twentieth centuries. These feelings are to a large extent justified, but several objections must be raised against the practice of constantly reviving old patterns. Period objects were originally created in a handicraft age; they were custom-built for people whose outlook upon life and society differed from ours in almost

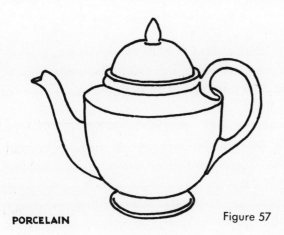

PORCELAIN Figure 57

every respect. The use of these forms today represents an artificial adaptation to bygone patterns of living, thus dangerously inhibiting the development of an adequate contemporary form. That such adaptation to period forms is indeed artificial is obvious in the "non-period" appearance of our bathrooms and kitchens. Here, newly developed habits of living have prompted the design of furnishings completely independent of period concepts.

The dangers inherent in this adaptation to period conditions become obvious when it is realized that most of the period pieces in use today are not handmade originals but machine-made copies. The two modes of fabrication—the methods of the craftsman, with his limited but skillfully executed and personalized output; and the processes of industry, with their mechanical power, scientific research, new materials, and mass-producing machinery—are intrinsically incompatible. Forcing the machine to imitate the craftsman's techniques, instead of utilizing the new shaping methods of which the machine is capable, not only produces wastefully but also drives a wedge between the means and ends of production and widens the chasm separating modern economy from our ideals of living. This chasm threatens the very existence of society. Our goal should be to close this chasm—not widen it.

Figure 58 represents the other group of contemporary tools for living. It is, to use the popular term, a "streamlined" vessel. Streamlined design—the unsatisfactory outcome of "functional design"—is the antithesis to the period approach to form. Whereas the period designer emphasizes the sentimental aspects of his product, the functional designer takes rationality to be the main forming factor of his work. Historically, functional design was a reaction against the inane monstrosities of the late nineteenth century. Sullivan's slogan—Form follows function—came as a revelation. The design formula implied in this slogan seemed simple enough: if the functional requirements of an object are sufficiently met, form will issue automatically. In this rational conception of form there is the influence of the engineer—at that time the most optimistic of men—who is satisfied when his machine performs the mechanical actions for which it was designed.

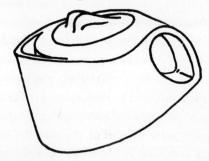

STONEWARE   Figure 58

This functional concept of form has restored some sense to many tools for living that have suffered from the hands of the Victorian designer; and the aesthetic appeal of ball bearings and transmission gears offers proof that satisfactory appearance may result from mechanical computation.

Closer observation reveals, however, that even such purely technical objects as gears are by no means completely defined by technological requirements. They always contain elements the proportions of which are established by nonfunctional decisions of "what looks better"; and with the growing complexity of a device, its design becomes more and more arbitrary. For example, the automobile demonstrates that functional considerations alone do not determine the product of the functional designer. Still, it might be argued that the shape of a purely functional device could be determined functionally by carrying all considerations of stresses and strains to the limits of our knowledge.

In spite of all the attention focused on "function," it is not at all certain that a purely mechanical device actually exists. The functional designer is seriously at fault when he forgets that in the final analysis it is not the solution of a limited technological problem but rather the satisfaction of the whole man that should be expected from his tools and devices. Unless man is degraded to a monstrous robot, his needs should transcend the computations of the engineer. What man expects beyond technological function is form, which is a quality that the technician cannot determine because it transcends rational considerations.

The story of "streamlined" design reveals the paradoxical compromises that have been forced upon the functional designer by the human need for form. Investigating the disturbance of air around objects moving at high speed, scientists discovered the streamline and found that a shape like a teardrop offered the least possible wind resistance. The teardrop shape as such was technically of quite limited significance. Even in airplane design its application involved the consideration of additional requirements that changed its basic lines. The vogue of streamlining that characterized the past decade or two did not result from functional considerations; instead, designers discovered in the streamline a symbol for speed, efficiency, and scientific approval. Delighted to have found a design idea that relieved them from guessing "what the public wants," manufacturers swamped the market with objects arbitrarily wrapped up in streamlined surfaces. The public responded by buying these objects, which, they thought, expressed the achievements of modern civilization with which they wanted to identify themselves. Functional considerations were rarely involved in this process: the streamline may have some justification on automobiles, but flatirons certainly move too slowly to be influenced by air currents; and floor lamps and teapots should symbolize the very opposite of fast movement. Yet all these objects, and many others, appeared in this new shape.

The fact that the streamline has been such a great success, despite its relatively meager content of meaning, illuminates man's need for form. Although the streamline may symbolize our fast-moving times to some extent, its application has certainly been exaggerated. The needs of the human being and those of the airplane are too far divergent to allow them to be subsumed under the same formula.

The period designer tries to preserve in his designs certain qualities of human significance. He attempts to achieve this preservation by not recognizing the social and technological changes that have occurred since his designs were originally created. The functional designer accepts the machine and the living conditions of the machine age; but he fails to acknowledge all the needs, desires, and aspirations that form the most human part of man. Both these designers offer only partial solutions. Contemporary form will result from a synthesis superseding these.

Figure 59 illustrates a contemporary pouring vessel that offers a satisfactory minimum of the new synthesis. This pot seems acceptable in the human sense as, for example, a symbol of a pleasant family breakfast; and it seems acceptable in the technological sense as the product of an honestly mass-producing machine technique. In other words, this vessel is correct on several levels. It is technically correct, because it meets the requirements of safe and easy handling, good pouring, and easy cleaning and storing. It is economically sound, because it uses methods of

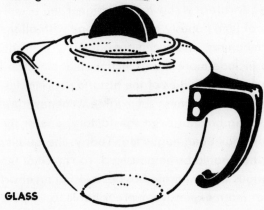

GLASS   Figure 59

shaping and assembling that are adapted to the machine process and because it uses materials—heat-resistant glass and plastics—that are easily mass-produced. It is aesthetically satisfying, because it combines an image of grace with an appearance of dependability, and because it uses contrasts of shiny and dull, transparent and opaque materials that, better than applied decorations, make it pleasant and stimulating to behold. Finally, it is psychologically correct, because the honesty of its material and formal features, economy of means, precision of line, and appropriateness of shape, all combine what man expects and what the machine can do.

The pouring vessel may seem to present only a small answer to the great problem of contemporary form. However, if it is accepted as a symbol of similar beginnings in housing, in equipment for home and office, in machinery, in transportation—and, by implication, in sculpture and other arts—then the trend of the new departure may be apparent. To consummate this departure in the new synthesis, three basic qualities are needed: awareness, honesty, and humility. Awareness shows the designer the ramifications of the form problem; honesty helps him cope with all the aspects of function, meaning, and technique; humility prevents him from wanting to include more than function, meaning, and material warrant. The good qualities of the historic pouring vessels discussed earlier derive from these same three. Whenever the form of any tool for living has not been satisfactory, one or the other of these qualities has been neglected. Today, the quality of humility is the one that should be emphasized. Too much of the tradition of unpretentious workmanship has been lost in an effort to make things appear more expensive, more reliable, and more satisfactory than can be justified by their innate quality. This intrinsically immoral tendency is, of course, part of the general deterioration of social relationships. If the synthesis of the new form could be achieved on the level of the tools for living, man would possess a foundation on which another generation could rely in their effort to achieve the loftier realizations of form that he so badly needs but does not own today. A high pinnacle needs a broad foundation. The conception and effective presentation of aspirations and ideals in what is traditionally known as works of fine art depend on a coherent cultural substructure, the form of which is realized in tools for living. This structure is broken; to mend it is a primary task.

Rhythm in Pattern

In addition to the concept of space as framework and symbol of form, determining such spatial realizations as sculpture and design for use, there is another equally fundamental concept that determines and expresses form—rhythm. Just as a concept of space establishes the scene itself, so does a concept of rhythm establish the way in which events in this scene are experienced. Rhythm suggests form as it applies to motion.

The concept of rhythm presents an aspect of form commanding particular interest today. Rhythm relates to movement, as movement relates to change—and change is the essence of a time of transition such as the present. Because of the necessity of continuous adjustment to these changes, it is often argued that form, being essentially static, cannot exist while these changes are in progress. This argument implies that more static conditions must exist before form can be established. However, tentative as static form may be today, rhythm does offer dynamic form for the processes of change.

Undoubtedly the transitional character of the present manifests itself in many traits that defy static form. Language, for instance, one of the most sensitive indicators of change, tends to give negative connotations to the term "static" and positive ones to "dynamic." The concept of progress is used more frequently today than it has been in the past; and on the development of transportation, we have spent more energy than any other generation. Formerly, the gait of the horse was the speed limit of locomotion. Now, railroads, automobiles, and airplanes have not only changed man's concept of terrestrial distances; they have also changed his concept of traveling. Today, a traveler is more interested in the ways of getting somewhere than in the places he intends to reach. Our highways and cars are more presentable than our cities and houses. "If it is better to travel than to arrive it is because traveling is a constant arriving, while arrival that precludes further traveling is most easily attained by going to sleep or dying." Thus John Dewey sums up the philosophy of a society in motion. Living habits reveal similar traits. Social life is shifting from the static home to the more dynamic hotel; office layouts and partitions in New York are changed on an average of every ten months; the stately cupboards and four-posters of our ancestors are being replaced by small, transportable, and even collapsible articles.

These examples of change indeed suggest that form, as it applies to states of being, must be somewhat tentative today. However, as it concerns individual man—who is in a perpetual state

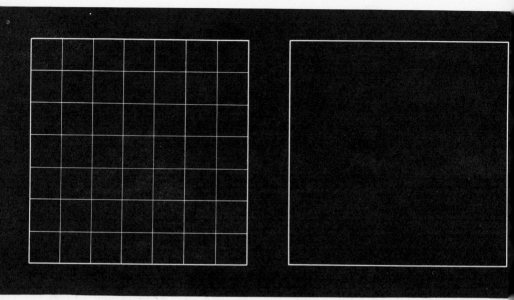

Figure 60
Figure 61

of change, who constantly alters his physique so as to make himself over every seven years, and who does this without ever losing his identity—form must apply to more than static existence, it must govern the very process of becoming.

Rhythm is generally recognized in motion, which in turn involves a sequence in time not present in a pictorial illustration. There exists, however, one type of visual art—the art of the pattern—that, although static in itself and thus pictorially presentable, does involve rhythm because it is experienced through the movement of the eye in registering impressions separated by time intervals. Awareness of the rhythmic form in patterns will lead to the appreciation of rhythm beyond the few illustrations offered here.

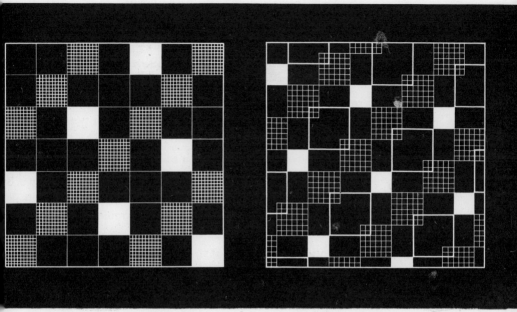

Figures 60 through 63 trace the development of a pattern and illustrate how a pattern functions. Figure 60, a plain surface, conveys nothing but stagnant emptiness. Figure 61 reveals a pattern that only slightly alleviates this emptiness—the effect of equal subdivisions is so obvious that it is understood at first glance. With figure 62 the beholder will feel that his interest has been awakened—it varies the basic pattern of figure 61 by stressing a sequence that enables the eye to discern a multiple design progressing in rhythmic fashion. These multiple rhythms are 1–1–1–1, 1–2–1–2, 1–4–1–4, and, if the pattern were extended, 1–8–1–8, and so on. The effect of this composite compares with that of a tone with several overtones: in both cases

Figure 62
Figure 63

there are no fundamental changes, but only enrichment. Still, this design is so obvious that it cannot sustain any lasting interest. Once this pattern is understood, it becomes trite. To keep stimulation alive, variations must be introduced to veil its basic consonance and to maintain suspense. Figure 63 shows such variation: its pattern offers repetition veiled by complexity. Here the movements can be enjoyed because they balance certainty with the stimulus of adventure.

An extended viewing of the pattern of figure 63 reveals that it too suffers from the mechanical and unvaried repetition of its design. This disappointment in strictly mechanical measures is justified. The human organism requires for its stimulation organic rhythms rather than mechanical beats; mere repetition is not enough. Even our heartbeat is not strictly repetitious, as the cardiograph reveals; its curve varies, **however** slightly, from beat to beat.

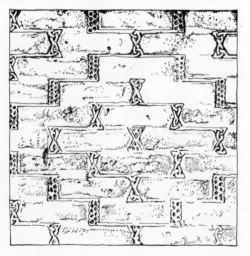

Figure 64

Figure 6

The creative artist, of course, senses this condition. When he designs a pattern, he follows organic impulses of composition and does not copy mechanical measurements. Although his designs are often susceptible to mathematical approximation, they will be distinguished by the slight variations from the rule that elude rational determination. Figures 64 through 67 illustrate the organic quality of such rhythmic pattern with a medieval wall décor from Asia Minor, a section of seventeenth-century Spanish grillwork, a piece of eighteenth-century French lace, and the front of a contemporary apartment building. The diversity of these three media indicates the great variety of ways in which pattern gives visual expression to rhythm. So manifold, indeed, are the applications of pattern, often covering every available surface of paper, metal, fabric, wood, and stone, that there must be recognized here a desire for rhythmic expression as all-pervading as concepts of space.

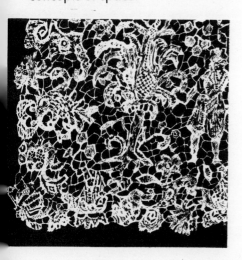

Figure 66

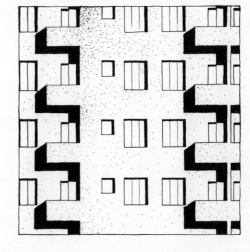

Figure 67

Along with the changes in concepts of space from period to period, it is only logical to expect to find similar changes in rhythm. The printed page offers a pattern with which we are all familiar. Its history will show to what extent this expectation is justified, and will also illuminate the relations between pattern and societal form.

Art in Printing

The pattern of printing has not been a part of Western civilization for as long as sculpture and pottery. Lettering by hand took its place until the fifteenth century. However, the introduction of the printing press does not interrupt the continuity of expressive adaptation. A difficulty arises, however, from the habit of looking at a book page for its literary content only—reading the page but not usually observing it. To counteract this rationalistic habit, I again suggest a more unitary approach. The foreign-language illustrations I have chosen will make it easier in this context to subordinate the meaning of words to the meaning of their visual pattern.

Because of the visual aspect of the book page, it may be asked whether, since the page is composed of words made up of letters, it is not the quality of these individual elements that determine the quality of the page as a whole. This is true to some extent, but proportions of print and margins and the spacing of lines and letters contribute elements to the pattern that are independent of the shape of the individual letters. The rhythm of a pattern, as I have already shown, depends less on the individual parts of which it is composed than on the order in which these parts appear. The individual letter thus plays a double role: it is the element from which the patterns of print are built, and it is a symbol of form in its own right.

Figure 68 reveals classical form in the stately pattern of a Roman inscription, cut in stone in A.D. 114. Figure 69 shows the vigor of the Romanesque in a parchment written about 1050 in a Rhenish monastery, an heir to what has been saved of the Roman tradition. Figure 70 shows two pages made in Germany and England, respectively, in the fourteenth century. Both are "illuminated" with brightly colored and gilded drawings. These illustrate, with the growing involvement of the pattern, the two phases of the Gothic age, the first aspiration giving way to anxiety.

Figure 68

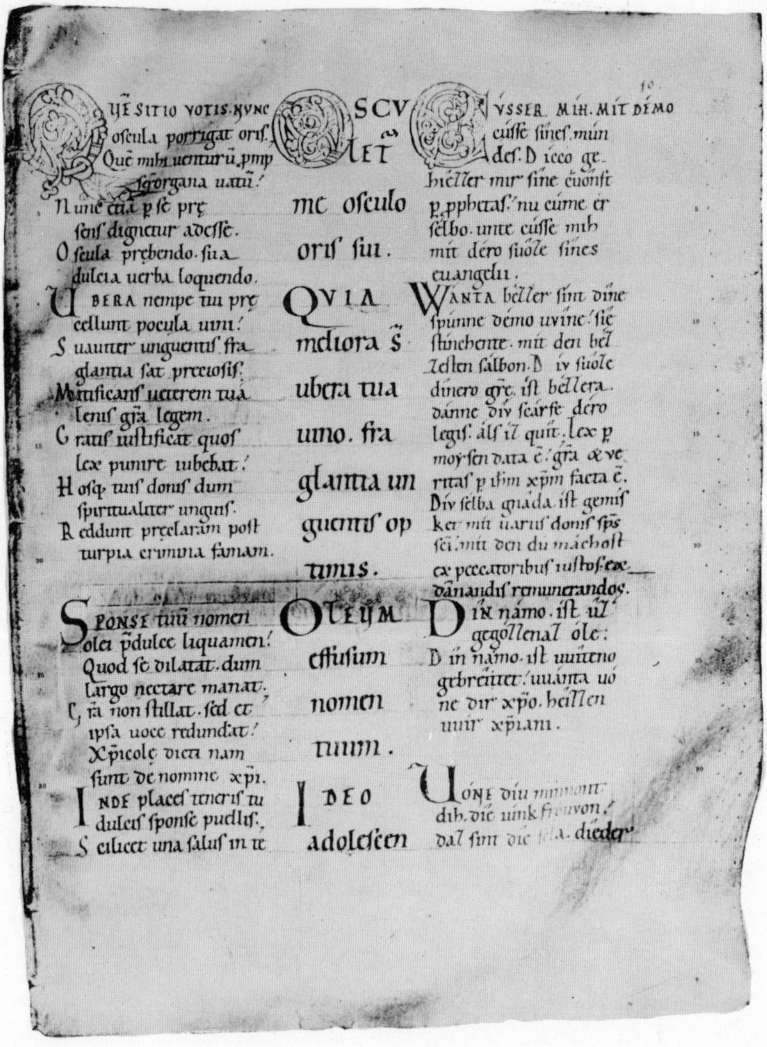

QUESITIO VOTIS. NUNC oscula porrigat oris. Que mihi uenturum promisit organa uatum! Nunc etiam per se presens dignetur adesse. Oscula prebendo. sua dulcia uerba loquendo. UBERA nempe tua precellunt pocula uini! Suauiter unguentis fraglantia sat preciosis. Mitificans ueterem tua lenis gratia legem. Gratis iustificat quos lex punire iubebat! Hosque tuis donis dum spiritualiter ungis. Reddunt preclaram post turpia crimina famam.

OSCULETUR me osculo oris sui.

CUSSER MIH. MIT DEMO cusse sines mundes. Dicco gehieller mir sine cuonft per prophetas. nu cume er selbo. unte cusse mih mit dero suoze sines euangelii.

QUIA meliora sunt ubera tua uino. fraglantia unguentis optimis.

WANTA beller sint dine spunne demo uvine. sie stinchente. mit den bezzesten salbon. Div suoze dinero gratie. ist bellera. danne div scarfe dero legis. als iz quit. lex per moysen data est. gratia et ueritas per ipsum christum facta est. Div selba gnada ist gemisket mit uariis donis spiritus sancti. mit den du machost ex peccatoribus iustos. ex damnandis remunerandos.

SPONSE tuum nomen olei perdulce liquamen! Quod se dilatat. dum largo nectare manat. Quia non stillat. sed et ipsa uoce redundat! Christicole dicti nam sunt de nomine christi. INDE places teneris tu dulcis sponse puellis. Scilicet una salus in te

OLEUM effusum nomen tuum.

DIN namo. ist ul gegozzenaz ole: Din namo. ist uuitteno gebreitet. uuanta uone dir christo. heizzen uuir christiani.

IDEO adolescen

UONE diu minnont dih. die iunk frouvon. daz sint die sela. dieder

Figure 69

In em fiur an der fiust
do geschuf der tiuuels list
Daz es in dem fiur
nach indes natur

Ward em chalb an d geschaft
dem nach der lewt solher chraft
Daz es got wär vñ sprachen so
mit frolichem mut do
Si ach der tiuuels gepot
israhel diz ist din got
Der dich mit helfleicher hant
pracht von egypten lant
Von deines landes grozer schlag
friu an dem andern tag
er achtens einen alter da
vñ opferten dem chalb sa
Vñ heten groz hochzeit
frolich gar an wider streit
Heten si sich gegeszet dar
nach der opfer saz die schar
Ze wirtschest mit az vñ tranck
dar nach ward mehtz ze lanck
Er daz si an dem selben zil
giengen frolich ze spil
Sach dem gepet vñ songen
si tanzten vñ sprungen
Als in nach grozer swær
grozziu lieb geschehen wær
ot zu seinem chnecht do sprach
do disew sünd geschach
Binck ab dem lewt gesünder hat
mir sünleicher missetat
Das sprach got in der wer also
als er sich ret erzaigen do
Vr vñ sprach daz lewte dem
in zorn nicht daz lewt mein
Got sprach la mich die schar
vertiligen vñ zerstörn gar

Durch du missetät vñ ich
zu grozzer diet mache dich
Nayn mht herr genad mein
ich pit dich tu tu mir schein
Genad vñ la deinen zorn
gen deinem lewt sei er verlorn
Vñ zün mht vnd diz geschicht
daz die egypten sprechen icht
Got hat si chündichleich
pracht auz disem reich
Do er het also gedacht
wurdens in die wust pracht
Daz er dann vor die schar
wän er gewalich gar
Wais er ze geben daz laut
daz dein schatz in hat benant
Sach ewinkleichem aygen recht
gedenck hie an deinen chnecht
In deiner genaden güt nu
dar nach bomens ze stimme du
Zu würens disiu selben lant
nach in ze geben in ir hant
o got in seiner güt
mit götleicher diemüt
Derzorns vnd der diu vgan
als er ze tun sich wa man
Vñ seinen zorn ab gelte
moyses von danne gie
Vñ trug die tauelen mit im dan
Iosue der rain man
Was do gen im gegangen
wan nach im begund in lange
Vñ hiet leicht aller tæglich
hin gen im gemachet sich
Er enpfieng in wol vñ was fro
mit einander giengen si do
Gen dem her dem perch ze tal
do si hnamen disen schal

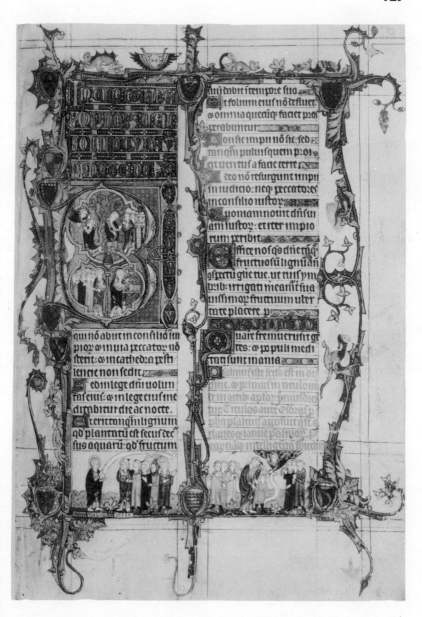

These few examples of medieval typography illustrate the rhythm of their time as it found expression in the patterns of lettering. Comparison with corresponding works of spatial art shows close similarities of proportion, suggesting that it is one and the same form that these different arts realize. Recognition of the formal qualities expressed by these patterns emphasizes the fact that the book functions not only in the capacity of distributing conceptual knowledge—as the intellectual believes who scans its pages only for their literary content—but that it also distributes rhythmic form. For the whole man, who wants both to read a book and to behold the pattern of its pages, the book becomes a vital part of the communal tissue, which to him must be more than a fabric of ideas—it must be a fabric of art.

During the fifteenth century the art of printing began to supersede hand lettering. The printed book became the vehicle for communication of ideas and rhythmic form. The thesis that form is a function of community rather than of its individual members is substantiated by the further development of handwriting. Before printing was introduced, the letterers of books conformed in the rhythm of their personal patterns with the objective rhythm of the community. During the fifteenth century, printers copied these handwritten letter patterns for their presses, as figure 71 shows, and they continued to use them as long as they harmonized with the rhythm of their time. Handwriting, thus freed from the responsibility of communicating form to the community, receded into private correspondence, losing its relation to this form. Figure 72 shows two letters, one written fifty years after, the other a hundred years after, the introduction of print. They illustrate how writing reacted to this loss: within a few generations it became amorphous.

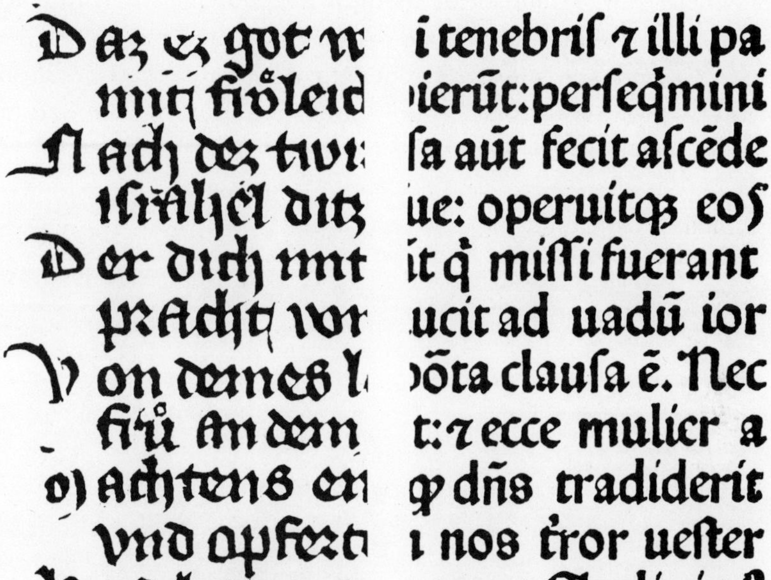

Daz es got w
mitz fiöleid
Nach der tivr
Isralhel ditz
Der dich mit
prachtz vor
Von deines l
siu An dem
o) achtens en
vnd opferti
Vnd heten g
fiöleich gen
heten si sich
nach der oz
Zewirtsthet
daz nach w
F daz si An de
giengen fur

i tenebris z illi pa
ierut:perseqmini
sa aut fecit ascede
ue: operuitqz eos
it q missi fuerant
ucit ad uadu ior
pota clausa e. Nec
t:z ecce mulier a
qz dns tradiderit
i nos tror uester
s terre. Audiuim'
is rubri ad vim
egypto:z que fece
ibus q erant tras
fecistis. Et hec au
uit coz niz: nec re
tu uestru. Dns.n.
elo sursu:z i terra

Figure 71

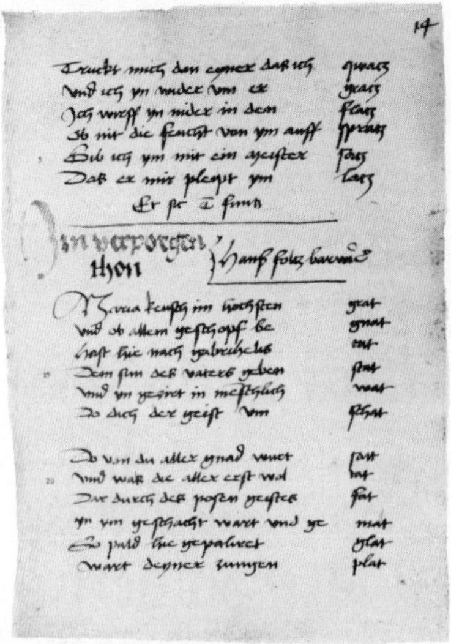

14

Trucket mich den eymer daß ich · gwatz
Und ich yn wider vom er · geatz
Ich wurff yn wider in den · flatz
Ob mir die feucht von ym auff · spratz
Gib ich ym mit ein meister · satz
Daß er mir pleybt ym · latz

Er sp̄r ī fins

In verporgen thon } Hanß Folz barwirer

Maria keusch im hochsten · grat
Und ob allem geschopff be · gnat
Hast hie nach gabrihelis · rat
Dem sun des vaters geben · stat
Und yn geziret in mesthlich · wat
Do dich der geist um · schat

Do von du aller gnad venet · satt
Und waß die aller erst wol · tat
Die durch des posen geistes · fat
yn ym geschacht wart und ge · mat
So pald hie gepalirt · glat
wart deyner zungen · plat

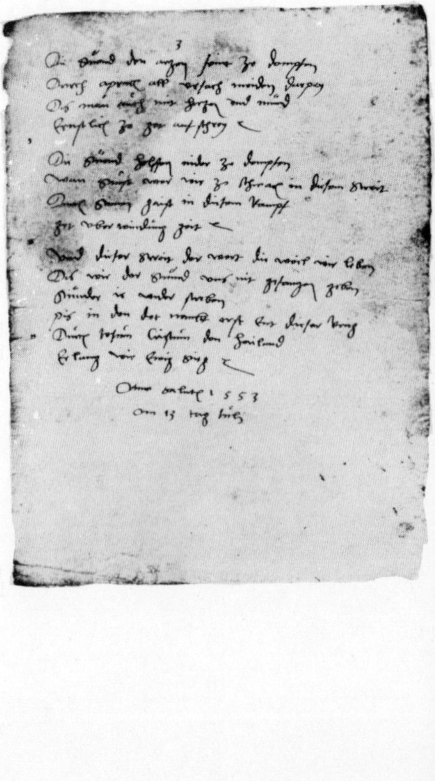

3

Anno 1553

Figure 72

Figures 73 through 78 illustrate a sequence of books through the intervening centuries to the print pattern of today. Figure 73, a Latin Bible printed on vellum by Jenson in Venice in 1476, illustrates the rigorous standards of well-proportioned form characterizing the Italian Renaissance. It also indicates aesthetic sensibilities that, in bookmaking at least, have not been surpassed. Figure 74, an example from the Netherlands, where the art of printing flourished during the seventeenth century, reveals the florid vitality of the high Baroque and also shows the vehemence known from the work of Rubens and other records of this period. Figure 75 illuminates the consummate grace and fragile refinement of the Rococo. This book was printed ten years before the French Revolution ended an aristocratic way of life and ushered in the modern age. In figure 76, a dedicatory page printed in the famous officine of Didot, there is the dry and correct classicism of the Napoleonic era.

The pattern of figure 77, from a book published at the turn of the twentieth century, pathetic in its desperate search for decorative beauty, shows rhythmic form at its lowest ebb. Comparison with figure 73, for instance, indicates the extent of this decline. I am reminded here of Baudelaire's complaint: "The value of time and money is so high. Materialistic activity leaves in the minds little room for better things (pour les choses qui ne sont pas de la terre . . .)."

Figure 78, an example of a new typography, shows how typographers of the 1920's tried to establish the pattern of a contemporary rhythm. Here the tide has turned, and a reawakened sense of responsibility toward form searches for expression. It is also noticeable, however, that this formulation of rhythm is more mechanistic than it is organic and unitary, thereby reducing the significance of the pattern. It is reminiscent of the schematic presentations of pattern discussed earlier and also of the mechanistic contemporary sculpture that leaves much to be desired.

Typography has not yet advanced beyond the suggestions of figure 78; the full realization of a contemporary rhythm in patterns of print has still to come. Most contemporary publications show at best a semiclassical pattern derived from William Morris's efforts of a hundred years ago. The screaming dissonance of visual matter in contemporary magazines shows how far one still has to go.

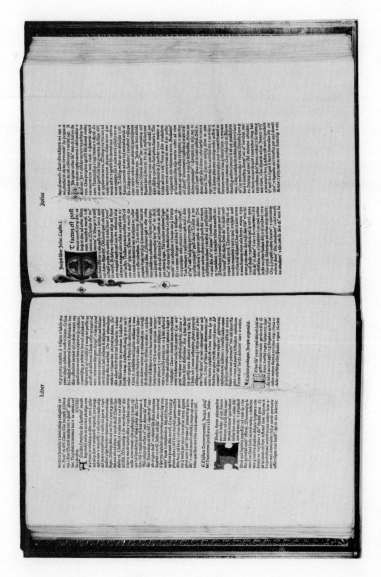

Figure 73

BOUTIQUE Vieh-Apoteck,
à
R E M E D E S,
Enseignant de quelle manière il faut preparer les medecines pour guerir les maladies des animaux.

Das ist:
Wie man heylsame Artzneyen / für mancherley Zufälle und Kranckheiten des Viehs bereiten soll.

A AMSTERDAM.

Pour Marc Doornick, Marchand Libraire sur le Vygendam, au Basil d'encre, 1672.
Avec Privilege pour 15 ans.

Getruckt und verlegt durch Marcus Doornick / Buchhändler auff dem Vygendam /
in dem Gantze Drattfaß 1672.

Figure 74

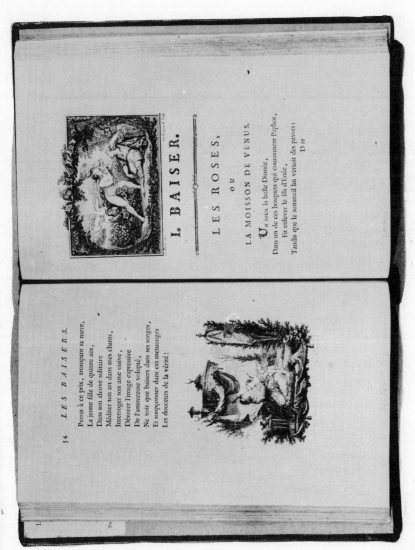

54   *LES BAISERS.*

Puisse à ce prix, trompant sa mere,
La jeune fille de quinze ans,
Dans son alcove solitaire
Méditer ton art dans mes chants,
Interroger son ame oisive,
Dévorer l'image expressive
De l'amoureuse volupté,
Ne voir que baisers dans ses songes,
Et soupçonner dans ces mensonges
Les douceurs de la vérité!

I. BAISER.

LES ROSES,
OU
LA MOISSON DE VÉNUS.

Un sou la belle Dione,
Dans un de ces bosquets qui couronnent Paphos,
Fit enlever le fils d'Inde,
Tandis que le sommeil lui versoit des pavots :

D iv

Figure 75

AU GÉNÉRAL

BONAPARTE,

PREMIER CONSUL

DE LA RÉPUBLIQUE FRANÇAISE.

PRÉCURSEUR DE LA PAIX, QUE L'ON DOIT À TES ARMES,
CE FRUIT DES ARTS NAQUIT DANS LE SEIN DES ALARMES:
SI, DIGNE DE RACINE, IL L'EST ENCOR DE TOI,
QUELQU'UN DE VOS LAURIERS S'ABAISSERA SUR MOI.
DE VOS NOMS RÉUNIS, ENFANT DE LA VICTOIRE,
LA FRANCE AVEC ORGUEIL CONTEMPLERA LA GLOIRE:
SES DESTINS SONT REMPLIS; LE FAVORI DE MARS
DÉPOSE SES LAURIERS DANS LE TEMPLE DES ARTS.
OUI, PRÉSIDE AUX TRAVAUX, ANIME L'INDUSTRIE;
FAIS D'UN NOUVEL ÉCLAT RAYONNER MA PATRIE;
ET PUISSENT TES EXPLOITS, QU'ADMIRE L'UNIVERS,
ÊTRE UN JOUR CONSACRÉS PAR D'AUSSI NOBLES VERS!

PIERRE DIDOT L'AÎNÉ.

Figure 76

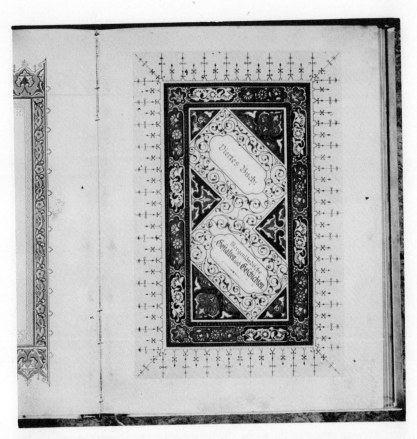

Figure 77

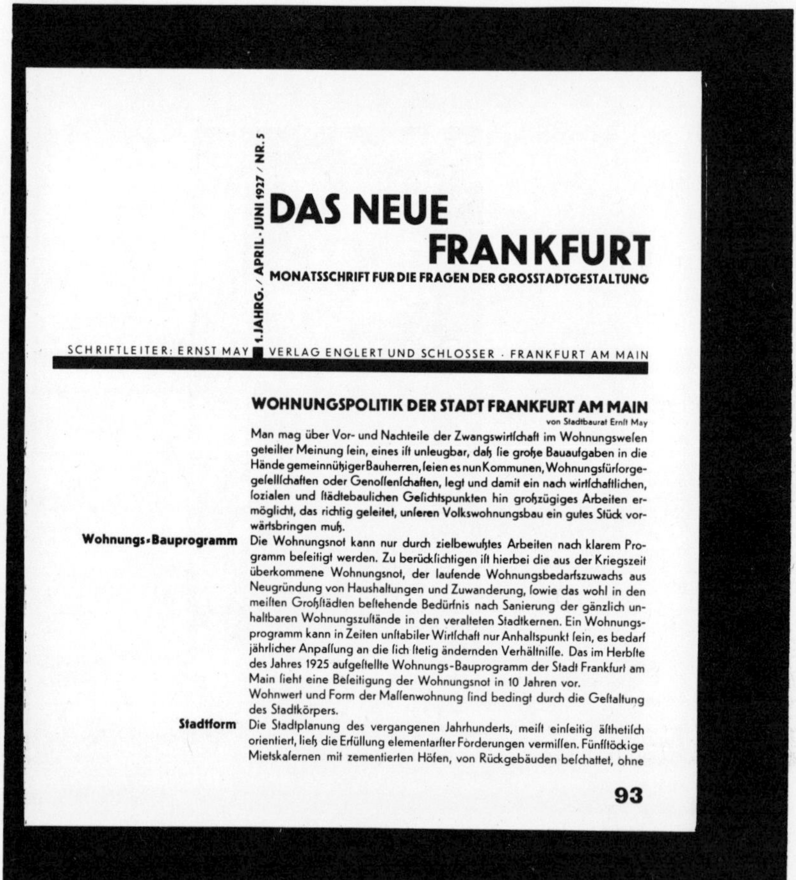

1. JAHRG. / APRIL · JUNI 1927 / NR. 5

DAS NEUE FRANKFURT

MONATSSCHRIFT FUR DIE FRAGEN DER GROSSTADTGESTALTUNG

SCHRIFTLEITER: ERNST MAY ▪ VERLAG ENGLERT UND SCHLOSSER · FRANKFURT AM MAIN

WOHNUNGSPOLITIK DER STADT FRANKFURT AM MAIN
von Stadtbaurat Ernst May

Man mag über Vor- und Nachteile der Zwangswirtschaft im Wohnungswesen geteilter Meinung sein, eines ist unleugbar, daß sie große Bauaufgaben in die Hände gemeinnütziger Bauherren, seien es nun Kommunen, Wohnungsfürsorgegesellschaften oder Genossenschaften, legt und damit ein nach wirtschaftlichen, sozialen und städtebaulichen Gesichtspunkten hin großzügiges Arbeiten ermöglicht, das richtig geleitet, unseren Volkswohnungsbau ein gutes Stück vorwärtsbringen muß.

Wohnungs-Bauprogramm Die Wohnungsnot kann nur durch zielbewußtes Arbeiten nach klarem Programm beseitigt werden. Zu berücksichtigen ist hierbei die aus der Kriegszeit überkommene Wohnungsnot, der laufende Wohnungsbedarfszuwachs aus Neugründung von Haushaltungen und Zuwanderung, sowie das wohl in den meisten Großstädten bestehende Bedürfnis nach Sanierung der gänzlich unhaltbaren Wohnungszustände in den veralteten Stadtkernen. Ein Wohnungsprogramm kann in Zeiten unstabiler Wirtschaft nur Anhaltspunkt sein, es bedarf jährlicher Anpassung an die sich stetig ändernden Verhältnisse. Das im Herbste des Jahres 1925 aufgestellte Wohnungs-Bauprogramm der Stadt Frankfurt am Main sieht eine Beseitigung der Wohnungsnot in 10 Jahren vor.

Wohnwert und Form der Massenwohnung sind bedingt durch die Gestaltung des Stadtkörpers.

Stadtform Die Stadtplanung des vergangenen Jahrhunderts, meist einseitig ästhetisch orientiert, ließ die Erfüllung elementarster Forderungen vermissen. Fünfstöckige Mietskasernen mit zementierten Höfen, von Rückgebäuden beschattet, ohne

93

Figure 78

I mentioned earlier that letters are not only the elements of print but are also symbols of form in their own right. In considering this symbolism now, it is necessary to abandon the consideration of pattern and to anticipate the discussion of pictorial art. Yet expressions of form overlap, and the experience with the imagery of letters may be considered as an introduction to the questions of symbolism that I will discuss more fully in conjunction with painting.

Figure 79 illustrates the history of the letter "A." These shapes are interesting in several respects. First of all, it is obvious that these letters indeed are symbols and that they evoke familiar conceptions of form. Notably, the bewilderment of the late Middle Ages (1488), the reasoned constructions of the Renaissance (1509), the self-assertion of the Baroque (1645), and the felicity of the Rococo (1770), are all qualities that have been indicated by capitals and sculptures. These resemblances again indicate that a specific form pervades all artistic expression of a given period. The letters of 1509 and 1805 also illuminate the specific interpretations the artists of the Renaissance and the classic revival have given to their longing after the classic Roman image. Another quality apparent in these letters is the continuity that underlies their modulations, thus pointing up the power of tradition. However, the changes involved also show that a living tradition finds expression in creative adaptation. The form of the letter "A" is weakest when it is based, not on imaginative development, but on submissive return to the past—as in the letter of 1805, which is an emasculated version of the Roman type; or in the letter of 1900, which is an unimaginative copy, lazy and without precision.

140

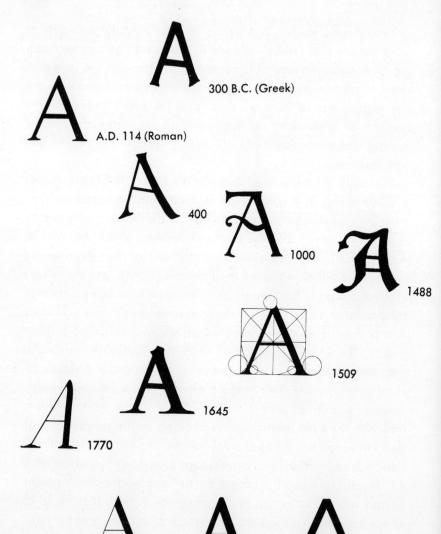

300 B.C. (Greek)

A.D. 114 (Roman)

400

1000

1488

1509

1645

1770

Figure 79

1805

1900

1925

The evocative power of these symbols is strengthened when they are composed into words. Figure 80 shows the word "life" stated in the letters of the last five centuries. The changes of form these word images suggest are so specific that I have named them.

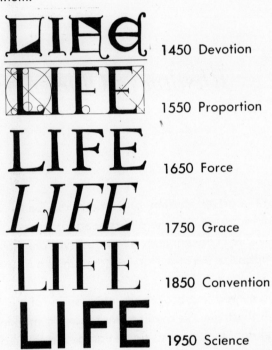

1450 Devotion

1550 Proportion

1650 Force

1750 Grace

1850 Convention

1950 Science

Figure 80

The story of symbolism in lettering thus seems to pause on a scientific, or rationalistic, note. Aside from some recent experiments with a contemporary typography, which have not yet found general acceptance, there is still no new typography that will offer both legibility and art.

Rhythm in Other Arts

Among the arts of rhythm, only poetry can be fully understood from printed notations; the others need instrumentations that are unavailable in this context. A few observations may help, however, to emphasize the importance of rhythm as a major factor of form.

Figure 81 shows a curved line broken up into a series of individual frames. It will illustrate the qualities that make a motion rhythmic and thus relate it to form. This figure can be interpreted in two ways:

Figure 81

It can be seen as a whole and interpreted as a shape; or it can be interpreted as the path of a moving point. In the second interpretation, it is clear that the point moves with a certain order: first it rises slowly above the horizontal, then it takes a plunge to a point below the center line, and finally it moves slowly back to its original horizontal direction. It so happens that the second half of this movement is the reversed counterpart of the first half. For this reason of inverted symmetry, this movement can be called a balanced one: it seems to be harmoniously concluded. At the same time, because the individual frames identify its steps, this movement appears to be a rhythmic one; and it is this quality of stepping from one frame to the other that here extends form into the dimension of time and into rhythmic change.

Figure 81 also suggests that the means the artist uses in creating the ordered sequence of rhythm is the timing of the changes he is planning. In figure 81, timing makes the changes come slowly at the beginning, quickly at the center, and slowly again at the end. The specific meaning of such timing, or the effect of rhythmic form, has already been indicated in the sound-wave experiments. It can now be described as resulting from the influence of the tempo of change in the image acting upon the tempo of nervous reaction. Rhythmic form, therefore, cannot be simply mechanical beat; it must result from a timing of changes controlled by the unitary qualities of the creative act.

An indication of the importance of rhythmic form in graphic art today is the fact that many painters no longer record their insights in single frames but create sequences of compositions, each of which represents a significant station in a continuous development. Figure 82 indicates this concept.

The best illustration of rhythmic form in pictorial art undoubt-

edly should be found in the moving picture. Yet, despite the interest in motion today, the motion-picture makers have not accepted the challenge of rhythmic form. With very few exceptions in the work of the avant-garde, the motion picture has remained a photographed stage show; it is essentially a canned version of the theater, an art quite different in aims and conventions from what the screen, the medium of graphic movement par excellence, should be able to present. This phenomenon is another indication of the lack of form in contemporary life.

Rhythm is not simply continuous movement. It implies the existence of fixed points in reference to which such movement can be registered. Points of departure and points of arrival are needed, and these points are expected not only at the beginning and at the end of the movement as a whole. As every step of a walk is a beginning and an end, so every change should be the end of the preceding and the beginning of the following movement. The fulfillment of these expectations involves complexities in rhythmical movement paralleling the complexities of pattern already observed.

Figure 82 illustrates the complexity created by the superimposition of several rhythms. First, there is a series of frames each of which encloses a complete composition. Second, there is a one-step rhythm; each of these compositions marks the beginning of a movement that links it with the succeeding one. Third, there is

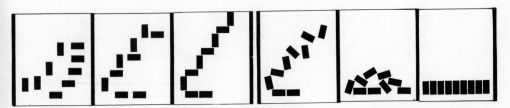

a three-step rhythm; positions 4, 7, and 10 emphasize the completion of partial movements. Fourth and last, the sequence as a whole presents a story with a beginning and an end.

The sequence of drawings in figure 82 adds, in the form of rhythm, the dimension of time to the two dimensions of graphic art. Interpreted as diagrams indicating successive positions of ballet performers, this sequence introduces the dance, an art that adds the time dimension of rhythmically controlled change to the three dimensions of sculpture. The dance is a very revealing art form and is particularly important in the context of this study, because the dance is concerned with the form of man's social relations on the community level more directly than most other arts. Also the dance is distinguished because it involves the actual or imagined participation of body as well as of mind. The dance, in short, is clearly an art of unitary man. It is for this reason that the laiks and carols of the Middle Ages, the measured pavane of the sixteenth century, the stately sarabande of the seventeenth, the graceful minuet of the eighteenth, the abandoned waltz of the nineteenth, the hectic fox trot of the twentieth, and also the elaborate folk dances of many countries, all reflect the realities of communal form more clearly, perhaps, than most other arts. It is unfortunate that there is no means of conveying here the spatial and rhythmic qualities of the dance; the experience of this art must be sought elsewhere.

The meaning of rhythmic motion can be clarified through a comparison of the dance with a sculptured pose. Figure 83 shows a dancer in a momentarily balanced and hence potentially static position. This balance is not mistaken, however, for the balance of sculpture; it is known that a series of movements has led up to this posture and that another series is going to lead away from it. This continuity of movement, only momentarily arrested at the point of this pose, is an essential part of the dancer's intentions. Traditional sculptures, by contrast, do not move; and the desire to imply motion in an arrested pose has often led sculptors into designing compositions in which it is nearly impossible to participate.

Figure 83

The Laocoön group, for instance, with its famed late-classic expression of agony that has puzzled art critics in past centuries, shows that a sculptor who mistakes arrested movement for potential movement is unaware of the essential form of his art. If he wants to formulate the meaning of motion, and not merely illustrate a passing instant, then mobile sculpture would be the answer to his needs.

Music, free of the implications of realistic storytelling that often veil the significance of other arts, mirrors most clearly the role of rhythmic motion as a vehicle of form. Because music is not a visual art, it is necessary to refer to its written language—unless, of course, there is opportunity to listen to it—to illustrate the relation of musical form to form in society. Although notes and bars are not music by themselves, they may serve here as visual substitutes for the rhythms they symbolize.

Figure 84 shows three musical phrases. The first one illustrates Gregorian chant. Here can be sensed the musical rhythm of the Middle Ages, which, like a growing vine enveloping a pillar, expresses the soaring transcendence of the cathedral. This rhythm is difficult for modern ears to grasp; in its pure spirituality it lacks the reassuring relation to the heartbeat of flesh and blood, which relation was established later by the Renaissance composers of the Netherlands.

The second phrase was written by Bach in the early period; the third, by Chopin in the closing period of what has been called the classic tradition of Western music. Bach's phrase is composed of four vigorous steps. The fixed points of this phrase and the eight-step movements connecting these points are so closely correlated and so rhythmically interwoven that they form a reliable structure, as it were, of suprapersonal objectivity. This phrase illuminates the consummate balance between freedom and law,

Figure 84

between worldliness and transcendency that distinguishes the form of the Baroque. Chopin's phrase, by contrast, shows little structural rhythm. It is personal, almost private, wistful, and romantic; it seems to float in dreamlike fashion. The objective form of Bach's music no longer controls the romanticism of subjective Chopin. There is also in Chopin's rhythms a note of pessimism and loneliness that forms a sharp contrast to the optimism pervading all Bach's work. Bach was sustained in this optimism, perhaps, by the assurance of a strong societal form in which he felt his own active participation. To Chopin's contemporaries, music was no longer a symbol of such communal form. It was a means of escape from hardheaded business and from the imperialism that had begun to engross their attention.

In terms of objective and subjective music, the development from Bach to Chopin parallels another development, significant for the status of the artist in his community—that from the craftsman who works on his commissions to the virtuoso who creates sensations through his self-expression. The implications of this development, which does not concern music only, will be discussed later, in connection with painting. In justice to Chopin, it should be added that underlying the obvious romanticism of his music can be felt the delicate beginnings of a new rhythmic order that later emerged in the works of Hindemith, Bartók, Berg, and other contemporary composers.

An over-all view of the period of Western music bounded by Bach and Chopin suggests that Mozart and Beethoven mark the halfway point in the general dissolution of objective rhythmical form. Post-Debussy music consummates this dissolution by managing often to move with a rhythm that is artfully contrived, or else by moving as formlessly as the ripples of a brook. Beethoven and Debussy represent the beginning and the end of nineteenth-century rhythmic development; it is not surprising that this development reflects the history of sculpture and design and, as will become apparent later, the history of painting. These parallels are not accidental; form in the arts and the form of society are cast from the same mold.

The following three sonnets, written in the sixteenth, nineteenth, and twentieth centuries, illustrate rhythmic form as it finds expression in poetry. Their melodies reveal movements linking arrivals and departures, welding words, thoughts, images, and sounds into rhythms that are part of the larger rhythm of their time. Shakespeare's sonnet has the objective, tightly knit, and reflective rhythm of the early Baroque. Elizabeth Browning's sonnet illustrates the subtlety of personal refinement as well as the difficulty of arriving at a generally valid form—both qualities characterizing the Victorian era. Prokosch's sonnet shows a determination, almost brutal when compared with the gentle efforts of the Romantics, to establish a rhythm commensurate with the need of form in the disordered flight of contemporary thoughts and feelings.

> When I consider everything that grows
> Holds in perfection but a little moment,
> That this huge stage presenteth nought but shows
> Whereon the stars in secret influence comment;
> When I perceive that men as plants increase,
> Cheered and check'd even by the self-same sky,
> Vaunt in their youthful sap, at height decrease,
> And wear their brave state out of memory;
> Then the conceit of this inconstant stay
> Sets you most rich in youth before my sight,
> Where wasteful Time debateth with Decay,
> To change your day of youth to sullied night;
>   And all in war with Time for love of you,
>   As he takes from you, I engraft you new.
>   (William Shakespeare)

If thou must love me, let it be for naught
    Except for love's sake only. Do not say,
    'I love her for her smile—her look—her way
Of speaking gently,—for a trick of thought
That falls in well with mine, and certes brought
    A sense of pleasant ease on such a day';—
    For these things in themselves, Belovèd, may
Be changed, or change for thee—and love, so wrought,
May be unwrought so. Neither love me for
    Thine own dear pity's wiping my cheeks dry:
A creature might forget to weep, who bore
    Thy comfort long, and lose thy love thereby!
But love me for love's sake, that evermore
    Thou mayst love on, through love's eternity.
               (Elizabeth Barrett Browning)

Shadow upon shadow, the shadow of love
    Fell on the naked sleeper at my side.
    A blue vein trembled and the midnight sighed.
"This," I thought, "is all I shall ever have.
    After this, nothing." And the wild thought drove
    All other thoughts out of my midnight brain.
"Nothing." The midnight ivy sang in the rain.
"Nothing but bone; nothing but rock; core; cave."

Women stood on a cliff far, far away
Praying the dead and dying; a waterfall
Rang in old Africa; and as the day
Gathered, I rose. Far down the pillared hall
Sobbing I found that other room where love
Lay waiting, even now, to comfort and forgive.

(Frederic Prokosch)

Poets, dancers, composers—and, to some extent, sculptors and painters—are at work today creating rhythms on the level of fine art. Unitary man wants these rhythms implemented on the level of practical accomplishment. On the level of recreation and entertainment, for instance, he expects sports and the motion picture to suggest rhythms that counteract the cacophonic chaos of man's surroundings and that help clarify the rhythm of existence. Furthermore, he expects city planners to give rhythmic order to traffic. Proper channeling of interurban, urban, and neighborhood traffic would apply the flow of rhythm he appreciates in music and poetry to the conditions of life in social interdependence. Factory and office offer similar problems awaiting solution.

Awareness of the importance of rhythm for a unitary life should lead man to harmonize the activities of modern life with his rhythmic requirements of work and leisure. Many of the dangers to truly civilized living that physicians, educators, and city planners are pointing out can be avoided when it is properly understood that all activity must connect with form through rhythm—otherwise, form becomes ineffective.

Architecture

Architecture consummates the integration of space and rhythm. These two modes of form are complemented in any actual instance by a third mode, which I shall discuss later—color. The suggestion of this combination of all modes of form in architecture is not verified by most buildings designed in the nineteenth and early twentieth centuries.

Undoubtedly it is easier to understand a Gregorian chant in a Gothic cathedral, a Mozart concerto in a Rococo salon, than in a nondescript Victorian concert hall. The relation of architecture to music is based to some extent on the consonance of rhythm and decor. Yet it is also based—and perhaps more strongly so—on the consonance of the musical rhythms and the rhythms of the architectural spaces experienced by moving toward them, into them, and within them. Architectural compositions are not single

153

units only; they form a sequence of correlated spaces that have meaning not so much by themselves as through their relation to each other. The introductory discussion of space offered a number of spatial formations that were comprehended by moving through them in the imagination. A more specific example of this rhythmic quality of architecture is given in figure 85, which shows the town plan of San Gimignano. The sketches illustrate in close sequence the way from the wall gate to the central church. This "walk" through a medieval town demonstrates, with the impact of a revelation, the truth that in architecture, as in all art, the creation of a single building or the statement of a single experience has little value when this building or this experience is not linked, as the sibling chain of the buildings of San Gimignano, in their chain of meaningful form. Contemporary architects have rediscovered this truth when they proclaim that city planning is a prerequisite for the revival of their art.

Architecture has been called the "mother of art." When the intrinsic significance of all the other arts is considered, it can be debated whether this one art should be singled out for such an exalted position. Still, architecture has a unique power to integrate the arts of a period into one representative symbol of form. It also has the potentiality of carrying the consummate expression of the meaning of social form. On the most personal level, architecture offers the framework for every kind of social intercourse in home, street, office, factory, park, theater, restaurant, or church. Except in the wilderness, we are never free of the formal suggestions of architectural surroundings.

In view of the importance of architecture as a symbol of civilization, it is especially disheartening to observe the atrophy of

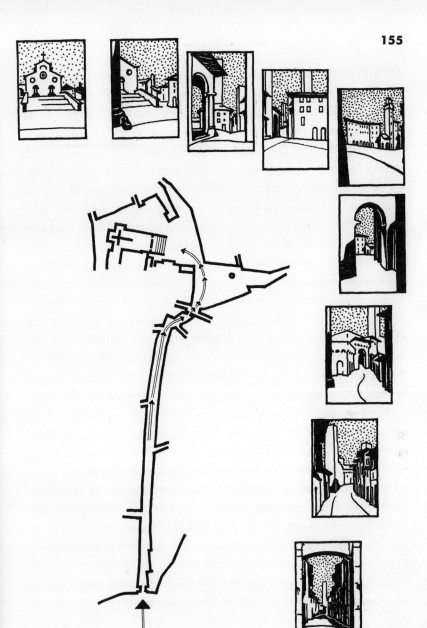

Figure 85

this art during the nineteenth century. By the end of that period it had nothing but façades and decorated surfaces to veil its emptiness. This shrinking of architecture into a mere school of the façade—a process almost unique in Western history—is partly the result of a lack of creative power, causing architects to rely for their designs upon volumes of scale drawings of historical buildings and parts of buildings. These volumes, of course, had been compiled by similarly unimaginative historians who could neither sense nor convey anything of their subject beyond the measurable facts of surfaces and ornamentations. However, in criticizing these architects who offered, instead of architecture, façades in "Tudor for colleges and residences; Roman for banks, and railway stations and libraries—or Greek if you like . . . French, English, Italian Gothic, Classic and Renaissance for churches . . ., Residences . . . in Italian or Louis Quince," as Louis Sullivan scathingly remarked, do not forget that the blame for this degeneration must be shared by a public that was willing to accept these substitutes for the realities of formed space.

The façade does not suffice as a representative image of the complexity of architecture. Like every other architectural surface, the façade is a mere explanation of the space-defining function of the wall. Similarly, no single room can be representative of an entire building. Rooms are the functional reason for the building's existence; alone, they are too static to reveal the rhythm of their spatial development. The architectural image most promising for this purpose is the staircase, which combines the static qualities of defined spaces with the rhythmic qualities of spatial movement. The stairway of figure 86, sketched while under construction, illuminates the power of architecture to integrate function, space,

Figure 86

and motion in an expression of form. Here the **sugge**sted form is particularly revealing because it does not take the beholder along the relatively static horizontal floor; instead it carries him in dynamic diagonals and rising curves through the width, depth, and height of the architectural medium.

The following figures show seven stairways with their architectural context. I have selected these particular stairways because each of them reveals the central problem—the achievement of integrated form characterizing the builder and his time.

Hatshepsut, Queen of Egypt, was determined to reconstruct her country and to resurrect its greatness, which had nearly succumbed to the devastations of the invading Hyksos. When she built the temple at Der-el-Bahri, she inspired this symbol of unflinching determination. As this stairway with incisive gesture imposes order upon the chaos of towering mountains, so the spirit of Egypt with the purity and strength of its single-mindedness imposes transcendent meaning upon the vagaries of individual existence.

This stairway leads into a temple: it is faith that transforms Egypt from a geographical concept into a historical continuum.

The Athena temple of the Acropolis is a sculptured monument. Its meaning lies in the outer volume rather than in the inner spaces, in the shape of its substance rather than in spatial relations to the temple's surroundings. This static quality of the temple precludes the suggestion of rhythmic motion. These steps do not invite the beholder into the temple; they merely form the pedestal on which the sculptural structure is erected.

The preoccupation with the palpable static aspects of substantial reality forms the core of Greek art and philosophy: the "glory that was Greece" began to decline at the time when Plato introduced the concept of the idea as a suprasensual object and the collateral concept of a relation between idea and matter. "Relation" for the Greeks had no palpable reality: a stairway that relates spaces had no place in classic Greek architecture.

Maria Coeli in Rome is a Medieval church. To Medieval men, who did not hesitate to express their acceptance of the realities of the hereafter, it was truly the house of the Lord. The desire to progress toward Him determined the values of their daily life; it also formed the essence of their art.

The men who built these stairs wanted to move closer to the "Kingdom of God, and His righteousness." They felt that in climbing these stairs they were performing a symbolic step toward their redemption from the sin that embraced all earthly existence.

The Scala Rotonda in the Vatican incarnates the spirit of the Renaissance. The men who built this stairway were no longer flee-ing from the wretchedness of this world. They had accepted it as their abode, and they intended to make it livable. They used their consciousness to plan it, their knowledge to order it, and their rationality to direct it.

These men decided that the world was a finite system of logical coherence and understandability. With this act they generated the scientific optimism that shed its terrestrial light on the succeed-ing centuries.

Michelangelo Buonarroti could not fully share the optimistic belief in the power of reason that marks the spirit of the Renaissance. His stairway of the Senator's Palace on the Capitol in Rome reveals the sense of tragedy that occupied his religious mind. As he moves toward his destiny, heavy with the burden of his doubts, he stops to ask of his God:

> "Certain of death, not of its hour . . .
> When, Lord, will Thou what they expect
> Give those who trust in Thee? Oh, this
> prolonged delay
> Destroys all hope and mortifies the soul."

And, hearing no answer, he moves on.

The staircase of the Bibliotheca Laurentiana in Florence breathes the wordly spirit of the Italian Baroque. The pleasures of collecting art and knowledge, the delights of social intercourse, the joys of good living, and also the consciousness that reflects and multiplies the value of those amenities—all find their expression in the interlacing rhythms of this architectural composition.

The nineteenth century had been dreaming of a world in which machines would do all the work; all that was left for man to do was to enjoy "the fruits of civilization." The present generation is awakening from this dream; and it feels invested with a new sense of responsibility. They have learned that the fruits of civilization can grow stale and rotten: they know that these fruits have to be grown and freshly reaped by every generation. They also have learned that, after all, machines are only tools, and that they need the planning mind and guiding hand of a master to make them build and not destroy the structure of civilization. Thus we have learned again to feel the need for the creative act that transcends mere organization—and that integrates knowledge and desire into a process of form.

This form must be a unitary one. It cannot be imposed from without; it must unfold from within—a plant must grow out of its soil. Many feel with Frank Lloyd Wright, the builder of these stairs, that architecture again may transcend eclecticism as well as engineering and offer the consummation of the new form. He is certain that "the new sense of depth that characterises architecture as integral . . . is a spiritual sense of the third dimension." But the responsibility for creating the spiritual climate in which this new architecture will grow—and with it the new form of civilization— rests with us all, the creators together with the beneficiaries of form.

Theater

In discussing and depicting works of art it has been unavoidable to show them as isolated factual objects. They could not be depicted as parts of the process of communication among people. Yet man's need for communication, both giving and receiving, is the essence of art—and works of art are only tools in this process. That words and drawings are better suited to describe facts than to clarify human processes has been particularly apparent in the discussion of music and the dance—arts that demand the participation of people for their realization. This dependence on men is greatest in the art of the theater.

The theater, using architecture, painting, poetry, music, the dance, and many minor arts, needs actors as well as audiences to come into existence. The central concern of the actor is to "get across the footlights"—and the response of the audience is his main reward. The theater thus presents in a concise symbol the idea of form through art. In Greek tragedy, where the chorus symbolically represents the audience at the scene of the drama; in the miracle plays performed among the crowds of the medieval marketplace; in the noisy participation of Shakespeare's first-night audiences; in the colorful processions enacting the meaning of the Church by and for their communities; in the pageantry that links the British with their throne—in all these, the art of the theater has been functioning fully. In what today we generally mean by theater or the stage, by contrast, we find manifestations of a Renaissance conception, a make-believe reality constructed behind a curtained proscenium that reduces the audience to isolated observers of an illusionistic outside world. This type of theater is in danger of being degraded to mere entertainment or being replaced by the movie house. The stage had a more vital function in society during the eighteenth century, when costume, scenery, and action on one side of the proscenium hardly differed from those on the other; and it is regaining its vitality in many contemporary experiments where the gulf between actor and audience is bridged by having actors perform from within the audience, as with Max Reinhardt; or by eliminating the picture-frame stage and offering "theater in the round," which tends to unite again the members of audience and cast in the unitary event of a work of art that exists as a bridge between men.

It is this web of human relations, this process of communication between men and groups of men manifest in the theater, that the reader must contribute from his own experience and imagination to works of art such as those depicted on the preceding pages.

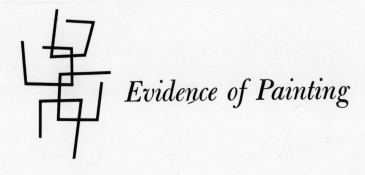

Evidence of Painting

Complexity of Pictorial Art

The pictorial medium has a particular complexity that exists in two ways. The imagery of painting is not so simple as the imagery of architecture or music. The mere fact that most paintings exist in terms of a spatial illusion—which makes one look through the picture frame—as well as in terms of a surface pattern—which makes one look at the canvas—indicates that the medium of pictorial art must be of unusual diversity. Then too, the role of pictorial art as a means of communication has been changing in the course of Western history to such an extent that the meaning of the word "painting" as it is usually understood today tends to mislead the beholder of Greek vase painting or medieval tapestries, Gothic stained-glass windows or Baroque church ceilings—or contemporary canvases.

The two aspects of pictorial art—medium and painting-beholder relationship—do not exist separately. The study of the ways in which the artist formulates his pictorial statements and those in which the beholder partakes of his work shows how painting functions within the framework of societal form.

My approaching pictorial art through an analysis of its medium requires an explanation, because it seems to contradict my intention to approach art through the unitary reaction of the whole man. Analysis—I cannot say this too often—does not usually result in any real appreciation of a work of art, the importance of which derives from its integral form, which must be grasped in its wholeness to be understood. Now with painting, the difficulty lies precisely in the grasping of this wholeness. Today most persons see only partial aspects of a painting: they see, for instance, only the illusion of an optical reality upon which the painter has opened the window of his picture frame. If this illusion does not gibe with the reality of their own visual impressions, they make allowance up to a point for "artistic freedom and temperament." Beyond that point they give up, simply because their preoccupation with recognition has not led to results.

Some kind of one-sidedness is characteristic, of course, of any cultural pattern. Perhaps men were particularly one-sided during the nineteenth and early twentieth centuries. Today, when man is enlarging the concepts of the last century, he must recognize the limitations of these concepts. He must take a more inclusive point of view toward the pictorial medium; he must give attention to the aspects of the medium that have not played an important role in paintings of the recent past. A survey of the meaning of various aspects of painting during other periods of civilization will facilitate this objectivity. It will also help in this context to relate painting to the other arts. Thus, my attempt to analyze the complexity of the pictorial medium should be considered only a means to the end of heightening the awareness of the unity of form in a work of art, and of emphasizing the relation of this specific form to the form of society.

Analyzing any painting, for example, "The Birth of Venus" by Botticelli, reveals that it exists in four different ways. Each observer's choice of the most obvious of these will depend largely on individual habits and attitudes. He may notice first a rectangular surface that, through the outlines of shore and horizon, of figures and fabrics, has been broken up into a pattern of specific rhythmic significance; he may be conscious of a color scheme the cool and crisp harmonies of which arouse a specific mood; he may notice a three-dimensional depth comparable to a stage set—from a distant backdrop several figures have moved forward to define the proscenium and create an impression of spaciousness for the event depicted; or, finally, he may recognize the subject matter or the story that the picture tells—Venus on her shell, exposed in her nakedness, with a robe being brought by an angelic attendant to rescue her from her virgin embarrassment.

In Botticelli's painting, these four factors that have been observed here separately—pattern, color, space, and story—are working together with about equal importance. They must be experienced together to create the specific impression of morning, youth, and hopeful beginning that makes "The Birth of Venus" so delightful to behold and that also makes it such a consummate representative of the spirit of the early Renaissance.

The decisive fact is that these four components of pictorial art have not been the same at all times, nor have they always been used together. It is these changes of imagery that make painting so complex and also make it desirable to consider the four components separately.

Pictorial Space

Works of art of a given period are closely related in their expression of form. It is therefore not surprising that changes in pictorial space parallel the changes in space concepts underlying three-dimensional art. Indeed, aside from some possible time lag, it would be difficult to imagine this to be not the case, since all art of a given time must spring from the same interpretation of reality. To illustrate concepts of pictorial space, I have designed a simple scene of houses, streets, and distant mountains, and have cast this scene into the space molds of certain periods discussed in earlier chapters.

Figure 1 depicts the space of Gothic pictorial art. It is essentially a vertical space: the Gothic artist overcomes the unwanted horizontality of perspective distance by several ingeniously devised means. He uses inverse perspective, the lines of which diverge rather than converge toward the visual depth; the up-tilted floor planes make objects appear above rather than behind one another; the shapes, overemphasized toward the top of the visual field, prevent them from receding into an illusion of distance.

This pictorial concept of a horizontally narrow but vertically elongated space is identical with the one encountered in Gothic sculpture, architecture, and philosophy. The resulting quality of pictorial "flatness" had distinct advantages despite—or rather because of—its lack of materialistic realism. It equipped works

Figure 1

of pictorial art with the quality necessary for them to coöperate with architecture through tapestries and stained-glass windows, with sculpture through painted panels, and with typography through illuminations and book illustrations. During the Middle Ages easel painting, in the modern sense of independent canvases, was still unknown; painters coöperated with goldsmiths, copyists, architects, and sculptors to realize a unified art.

With the advent of the Renaissance, pictorial space changed. Paralleling the trend of the times, painters gradually abandoned the objective transcendence of medieval space and arrived at the egocentric concept of the individual observer. They approached what might be called the specific space of the photographic camera—a space that carries the illusion of material reality but that is actually true only for the one individual observer who has his eye at the point from which the picture has been "taken." Figure 2 illustrates this new concept of pictorial space. The "reality" of this space is apparent when the eye (preferably with the other eye closed) is kept opposite that point for which it is designed—the doorway at the end of the street. If the eye is moved, for example, to the child in the lower left-hand corner, the composition as a whole begins to stare into a foreign distance. This space was invented at a time when man discarded the social continuum of the Middle Ages and introduced modern individualism; it is an individualistic space. This concept helped free painting from its relations to the other arts and gave it independence. As the artist exploited the possibilities of mechanical perspective, he no longer saw the working surface as part of a wall or a sculptural object. Instead, this surface became the canvas that existed only as a vehicle for his personal statement. This alienation marks the advent of easel painting as it is known today.

Ironically, as the objects depicted gain a kind of reality, the canvas loses it. The canvas becomes a screen, comparable to the ground glass of the camera through which a scene is to be viewed. As some wit has remarked, the reality of a painting shifts from the picture surface to the picture frame. The frame assumes, indeed, the function of a window opening on a vista. Notice that you look at the page in figure 1, whereas you look through the page in figure 2.

The shift from an aperspective, surface-related space to a

Figure 2

perspective space that is illusorily "real" implies a shift in the beholder's attitude toward painting. Surface-related space integrates a painting with its surroundings, and thus involves painting, environment, and people in a process of coexistence. Perspective space, existing only for the individual point of view, singles out both painting and beholder and emphasizes a chasm existing between the self and his environment—a chasm that can now be bridged only through observation. It is interesting to note that this shift in space concepts goes hand in hand with a shift from symbolism to realism in subject matter. Both seem to connect with the alienation between individual and society characterizing the Renaissance and finding strident expression in the writings of Machiavelli. As the individual becomes supreme, he also becomes lonely. These implications will be discussed at greater length in a later chapter.

Observe that the transition between the two extreme concepts of figures 1 and 2 has not been a sudden one. Its achievement occupied the artist for several centuries, and it cannot be described as a simple progression from one concept to the other. The Baroque, for example, achieved what may be called a synthesis between the two extremes. In figure 3 the same street scene as in figures 1 and 2 is stated in terms of the pictorial space that was developed, on the basis of Renaissance accomplishments, during the seventeenth century. Here the laws of perspective are applied; but the space does not extend into infinity, as it does in figure 2, nor is it as open toward the beholder. There seem to be a front and a rear limit, which enclose an amount of space and establish it as a unit in itself. The space structure of this composition, emphasized by a self-centered dynamism, suggests that

the event depicted has reasons for existence not exclusively centered in the beholder. The beholder is free to observe whatever
happens in this space, but he feels that these events do not depend on his personal attention. They seem to take place in harmony with some law that includes but transcends the beholder's
personal existence.

Because of the finite character of its space this picture can be
easily imagined as harmonizing with an appropriate architectural setting. Actually, the Baroque was the last great period of
art in which architecture and painting, together with sculpture,

Figure 3

formed a perfect union. The reason for the close relation of the Baroque pictorial concept of space to the space of architecture lies in its dynamism. The space of figure 2, which is foreshadowed by Renaissance painting and fully developed by the naturalists of the nineteenth century, is static: the beholder need only stand still and observe. The Baroque space, however, calls for active participation. Only through empathic exploration of the movements suggested by the painter can the meaning of this space, which is fundamentally not a fact but a process, be grasped.

With the end of the Baroque period, the pictorial concept of space developed rapidly into the "naturalistic" one of mechanical perspective. The painter became concerned mainly with calling attention to a specific observation he has made. Figure 4 records two such observations, different in story content but projected into the same spatial setting as figure 2.

Figure 4

As the beholder "reads" these stories, he notices that he is not concerned with an event happening on the page, in black and white; he is concerned with something happening outside on a street.

Beginning with the end of the nineteenth century, efforts were made to regain the artistic potentialities of pictorial space. These efforts have led artists to recognize again the reality of the pictorial surface, and have also caused them to doubt that easel painting is the only valid means of pictorial expression. Painters again have drawn tapestries, pottery, and architectural surfaces

Figure 5

into their orbit. Figure 5 shows the street scene of the preceding illustrations transformed into one expression of the new surface-related space. This expression is somewhat mechanistic in character, but so are many other artistic efforts of the early twentieth century. Despite this limitation, this composition is not necessarily restricted to its individual frame and to an individual point of view; it may well be integrated with surfaces of ceramics, textiles, or buildings.

Figure 6 hints at another, more unitary, expression of contemporary pictorial space. This concept transcends static realism.

Figure 6

Together with contemporary physicists—who have recognized the seeming reality of man's static space to be an illusion of the self-centered mind, and who have established the process of becoming as the main function of the space-time continuum—painters are beginning to work with a space that does not lend itself to static observation. Unlike the "given" space of the Renaissance or the nineteenth century, this new space gains existence only through the unfolding of events. These events, occurring singly or simultaneously in groups, create, in the act of their becoming, progressive spaces out of the chaos of nothingness.

Grasping this new concept of pictorial space is difficult for the beholder wanting to maintain the supremacy of the individual who figuratively finds the world at his feet. It is apparently not through observation that this space can be conquered; only through participation in its events can the beholder hope, not to conquer it, but to become a meaningful part in a coöperative effort.

Color

Color contributes to the expression of meaning in all visual art. Architects, sculptors, and designers employ color as a part of their language of form, whether it is inherent in the materials used or applied as a coating. In painting, color helps define space—colored areas visually move into or out of the surface according to the aggressiveness of their hue; it helps also establish a pattern—spots of related hue lead the eye through the rhythm of a composition; and color helps describe subject matter—blue sky and pink flesh emphasize the painter's intentions. The main function of color in painting, however, is the definition of mood. (There remains the possibility that colors carry symbolic significance. Modern man is not accustomed to such implications, but in medieval painting, for example, the coat of St. Mary was always blue. Anthropologists may discover some

day that what we feel about colors today derives from some definite meaning with which they were endowed in the distant past.)

The mood of a painting derives from its color harmonies or
chords. These, like chords of music, are composed of individual
sounds or hues carrying specific qualities of their own. In a painting, these individual qualities of hue interact and thus give expression to an emotional climate. The discussion of color is simplified by the fact that colors, unlike space concepts, patterns, or
images, form a closed system not unlike a double cone. Its base
is a ring formed by red, orange, yellow, green, blue, violet, and
thence back to red. The tips or ends of this system are black and
white, its center is median gray. From the three primaries in this
system—the corners of the triangle yellow, red, and blue—all
other hues, with the eventual help of black and white, can be
derived through mixing. (Optically speaking, the color system
may also be conceived as being based on two pairs of oppo-
sites—red and green, yellow and blue—which gives the cone a
square instead of a triangular structure.)

The attempt to describe the meaning of these individual hues
is a questionable procedure, but the theoretical character of the
color cone invites comparison with concepts of character traits or
behavior. Because no generally accepted psychology of color
exists, the following represents only the tentative result of some
limited experiments. According to these tests, pure yellow induces
an association with sheer energy; pure blue, with inert existence;
pure red, with latent potency. None of these three qualities can
enter by itself into the reality of action; it requires the medium of
mixture. Admixing the impulsion of yellow to the potency of red
produces the aggressive vehemence of orange. Adding active

yellow to passive blue results in the quiet activity of green. The addition of red to blue—potency to passivity—results in purple, a color suggestive of introverted recollection.

The ring of intense colors thus circumscribes symbolically the orbit of man's emotional attitudes, and also corresponds in its oppositions with the polarities of emotional states. Extrovert yellow opposes contemplative violet; inert blue opposes aggressive orange; active green opposes the latent potency of red.

At the still center of the color system lies median gray, symbolizing absolute neutrality. Around it there are hues of more complex mixture that do not seem as "unnatural" as the purer ones. They are partly neutralized by contradictory values and are thus more immediately reflective of the tensions and frustrations of human experience. Above and below the plane of pure and neutralized hues, color of reduced saturation corresponds symbolically with a reduced potential. Advancing toward white, there is, for example, in pink a weak dilution of the potentiality of red. Advancing toward black, brown, for example, seems sluggish when compared with the activity of orange.

Except in laboratory experiments, hues are never seen by themselves. They always appear in conjunction with many others, and the color chord thus perceived has a specific meaning that differs from the meaning of the individual hues involved. This is particularly true since hues are seen to change considerably according to the context in which they appear—thus, gray looks greenish against a red background and yellowish against a blue one. Also the contrast between two adjacent hues—say, red and green—creates a tension that, although clearly part of the total impression received, is inherent in neither the red nor the green.

Composition of these hues and chords leads to the color symphonies of painting. We have been made so conscious of the unique qualities of painters and paintings that it is difficult to abstract from the multitude of individual statements of mood the tenor of a typical color harmony or palette portraying the general mood that must have pervaded the social form of any given period. To avoid involvement in individual works of art, I have assembled abstract composites, shown in figures 7 through 11, of the hues most commonly used by the painters of the time in question. Although the striated arrangement of the hues is an arbitrary one, I think that the moods evoked by these illustrations approximate the mood expressed in the paintings of their time, and also that they are in discord with the pictorially stated moods of other periods. These charts illuminate the particular preferences of the painters of a certain time for some segment of the over-all possibilities of the color system. Their selections reveal the emotional climate of the society in which they lived.

Intense yet transparent, neutral in earthly hues of brown and green, ardent in blue and red that meet in purple, Gothic color expresses sensual pleasures transmuted by the fervor of spiritual directives. Here Gothic man is revealed as intimately aware of his existence in a God-centered world (figure 7).

Cool and detached, rich in variation but hovering around the neutrality of gray, the color scheme of the early Renaissance shows the painter, not blind to sophisticated enjoyment but wary of emotional commitments, setting out to describe "man and the working of his mind" (figure 8).

Inclusive in its palette, and with every hue warmed by the glow of a muted orange, Baroque painting reflects the sonorous earthy sensousness of its time. "Colors in painting," says Poussin, one of its masters, "are as allurements for persuading the eyes, as the sweetness of meter is in poetry" (figure 9).

Rococo color maintains and even enriches the harmonies of the Baroque. But its mellowed chords turn away from dark intensities and reach, through fading pinks and honey yellows and light blue-grays, toward the cool subtlety of a frail whitishness. Here are wisdom and tenderness, fragility and grace (figure 10). One might almost compare the mood reflected by the last four illustrations with the naïveté of childhood, the wariness of adolescence, the self-assertion of maturity, and the cautioned wisdom of advanced age.

Figure 11 reflects the glaring brilliancy of modern painting. Beyond a tendency to reach for extremes and explore intensity, no new theme expressed in a prevalent harmony can as yet be discovered. The stridency of these colors, no doubt, abandons the harmonies of the past. But this results not from cynical destructiveness, as some critics will have it: the mood here is too clean and positive for that, the chords uncertain perhaps but optimistic. Painters who compose hues like these are not looking back upon an end; they are looking forward to a new departure.

Figure 7

Figure 8

Figure 11

Figure 9

Figure 10

Pattern and Subject Matter

As space and color provide the stage, pattern and subject matter enact the story of the painting's message. These two often act together, yet their methods of communication are poles apart. Pattern in art, as I have shown, relates closely to rhythm, affecting man directly in his subconscious and in his emotions. Thus it resembles the rhythm of dance music in that dancers easily and subconsciously follow the beat without necessarily recognizing the music itself. Subject matter in art, by contrast, appeals to recognition. First, the critical mind has to observe what has been depicted; only then does it permit a reaction to what has been seen. This contrast between pattern and subject matter thus recalls the earlier discussion of the contrast between participation and observation. To some extent man is always both participating in patterns and exercising critical awareness, which is the reason

195

why both subject matter and pattern coexist in most paintings. These two elements are not always presented with equal strength, however, and it is the shift of emphasis from the one to the other that should be observed in this context.

Recognizing art as an expression of societal form, and recognizing the individual as being suspended between allegiance and revolt in relation to this form, the beholder should discover in the strength of a painter's patterns an indication of the strength of his participatory involvement; in the freedom of his subject matter, an indication of his freedom as a critical bystander. In other

Figure 12

Figure 13

words, periods of strongly integrated form should have created strong patterns and made the subject matter fit it; periods of weak or disintegrated form should reveal the corresponding independence of the individual by producing weak patterns subordinated to the "naturalistic" freedom of the subject depicted.

Figures 12 and 13, showing sections of two Greek vase paintings, may help substantiate this theory. A strong rhythmic pattern entirely dominates the story in figure 12, taken from a vase of the eighth century, a period of communal existence among the Greeks. In figure 13 the dominance is shifting toward the subject matter. The pattern is weakened, and the story is "getting out of hand" rhythmically. This illustration comes from a vase of the fifth century, a time when the communal pattern had begun to break up and critical individualism was taking its place.

The patterns of easel painting differ from over-all patterns in one important respect. Over-all patterns carry the eye indiscriminately over a virtually unlimited surface; pictorial patterns are finite. The painter composes them so that they keep the eye moving within the given frame, leading the spectator from some dominant point of departure to the edge of the picture area; thence back through the composition to some other edge of the frame; and finally—or rather repeatedly during the process of participation—to one or several focal points around which the pattern has been built.

The following drawings trace the main patterns of typical paintings from the Middle Ages to the present. They are intended to illuminate two aspects of pictorial pattern; its expression of specific form—inviting comparison with corresponding expressions in print, sculpture, and other arts—and its relative strength

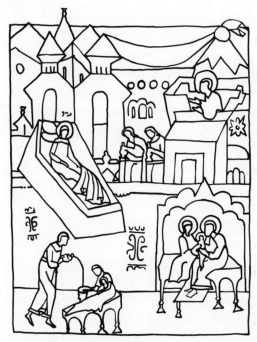

Figure 14

as expressed in the control these patterns exercise over the subject matter delineated.

Figures 14 to 16 offer three examples of medieval composition, ranging from early Romanesque to late Gothic. Corresponding with the closely knit communal form of the respective societies, the stories of these paintings are dominated by pattern. This pattern, however, undergoes revealing changes. In its angularity and strength, the pattern of figure 14 holds the promise of profound certainty. Deriving from the Byzantine, it relates to the well-knit order and assurance of a monastic and knightly way of life. In figure 15, the youthful angularity of the preceding pattern

Figure 15

Figure 16

has grown into rounded maturity. The drawing reveals a refinement and gentility that temper the earlier vigor. Yet although it is less "hard," the pattern of figure 15 carries an assurance of its own by showing a breadth of concept and an enveloping fullness.

Figure 16 shows a pattern that intimates changes in the broad security of the earlier Middle Ages. The pulse of its rhythm seems faster; its tightness implies an anxiety. This anxiety is relieved, however, through a vertical extension that relates this pattern to other expression of Gothic form and indicates the transcendent character of the Gothic quest for certainty.

Figure 17

Figure 18

Figure 17 reveals the relative weakness of pattern characteristic of the Renaissance. The outlines of pictorial areas add up to
descriptions of figures and spatial objects much more conclusively
than to an illustration of rhythm. Pattern seems to be only the
static description of ordered arrangement. This lack of a rhythmic
pattern reveals the self-centered, critical attitude of Renaissance
man, who wants only to observe and to know. "That painting is
the most praiseworthy," says Leonardo da Vinci, "which is most
like the thing represented."

With the beginning of the Baroque in Venetian painting comes
a revival of rhythmic pattern. In figure 18 there is the stirring of a
new beat—"an undulating form, one that resembles a flame,
animates the contours, and lends them nobility, elegance, and
truth," as Antoine Coypel said in 1720. The new pattern, however, seems still subordinated to the Renaissance concept of pre-
senting a tableau vivant to the discriminating bystander.

The high Baroque, as figure 19 shows, returns to the full participation of pattern in the pictorial composition. Here the event
of the angel's appearing to Christ is not depicted by itself: it
actually takes place in the beholder, who is drawn into the rhythm
of this flaming pattern. "The unique effect cannot be described,
it must be experienced . . .," says Nicolaus Pevsner of another
example of Baroque art. Thus, it may be said that Baroque art is
again an art for a community.

The nineteenth century produced paintings that, as figure 20
shows, outdid Leonardo in their emphasis on the "thing represented." In this almost photographic naturalism there is no recog-
nizable compositional pattern whatever, which is not surprising
when it is remembered that society then was correspondingly

Figure 19

Figure 20

weak in communal qualities. The asocial slogan of the survival of the fittest was in great vogue, and sensitive souls retired into a private romantic world of their own. William Wordsworth was moved to complain:

> O friend! I know not which way I must look
> For comfort, being, as I am, oppresst,
> To think that now our life is only drest
> For show: . . .
> The wealthiest man among us is the best:
> No grandeur now in nature or in book
> Delights us. Rapine, avarice, expense,
> This is idolatry; and these we adore. . . .

The nineteenth century, in short, left the individual little chance to participate in a community. Painting of that period reflected this development by degenerating into illustration.

The turn of the century brought the reversal of this trend toward anarchy. Artists, in advance of their shortsighted contemporaries, took the initiative and proclaimed a new departure. As early as 1878, James Whistler said: "As music is the poetry of sound, so is painting the poetry of sight, and the subject-matter has nothing to do with harmony of sound and color." From Whistler's time onward, painters have not ceased to invite participation through their endeavor to reëstablish the pictorial pattern. Some of these new patterns betray the eagerness, observed earlier in sculpture and typography, of constructing the new pattern rather than letting it grow. Figure 21 illustrates this constructivist tendency.

In the pattern of figure 22 there is a noticeable advance toward the more unitary qualities of gestation and growth. This pattern shows little of the felicity of the pattern in figure 21. But this felicity is a constructed one—it has the beauty of geometry. Controlled too rigidly by the mind, it achieves serenity at the expense of not taking fully into account the whole man with all his contradictions. The pattern of figure 22 seems closer to the whole truth—it contains violence and even despair. Yet with all its honesty, it manages to suggest the possibility of a new order that includes and

Figure 21

Figure 22

overcomes, rather than dismisses and negates, the difficulties of human existence.

The pattern of figure 22 is not perfect—it has holes in it, it has harshness of sound, it has contradictions. But despite the short-comings, it shows the possibility of a contemporary pattern—it signals a new beginning, a new growth of unity.

In the patterns of figures 21 and 22 the beholder recognizes a table, and a chess board, a hand, a shoe, a bottle; but these ob-jects are comparatively unimportant in this context. Twentieth-century painters do not follow Leonardo's dictum and work to capture the likeness of things. Facts, these painters may argue, are so well known today from "realistic" paintings and photo-graphs that there is no need for reiteration. The facts exist; the task then is to show how they hang together, what sense they make, where the meaning lies behind all these single, unrelated things. Painters reach this meaning through the integration of their subject matter with the rhythms of their pattern.

Seen in the light of history, the contemporary schism between schools of realistic or subject-matter painting and nonobjective or abstract painting thus seems to consist of a struggle between the two halves of a whole. The apparent overemphasis on nonobjec-tive qualities in contemporary painting is explained in the over-emphasis on descriptive realism that controlled painting one or two generations ago and all but obliterated the artist's concern for anything but the objects and scenes he depicted. A pendulum has to swing from one extremity to the other before it assumes a central position. It is perhaps in the work of Paul Klee that the new balance between pattern and subject matter is most conspic-uously in evidence. Figure 23 shows one of his conceptions.

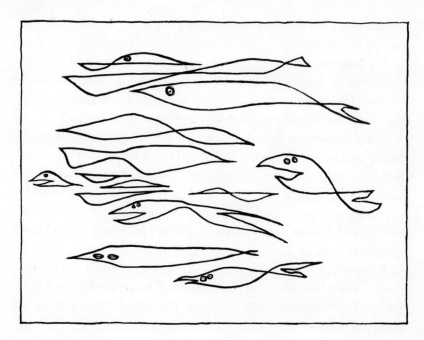

Figure 23

Subject Matter and Symbol

There is one other aspect of subject matter in painting that should be discussed in this context. It concerns the transcendence of descriptive reality through symbolism. When the subjects or events depicted by a painter are considered in the materialistic sense preferred during the nineteenth century, they are either illustrations of stories, of which the beholder is thereby reminded; or they are fingers pointing at realities to be reached by travel or adventure, by studying unfamiliar aspects of civilization, or—as in painted flesh—by circumventing the codes of morality. There exists, however, the possibility—if the observer has not entirely succumbed to positivist naturalism—to see in objects and shapes a portent of things beyond the grasp of crude realism. Thus a meaning may spring up at the sudden recognition of an expression of the hopes or fears of imagination, the loneliness or togetherness of childhood—exiled by our pragmatic selves. An object thus recognized—with an awareness that transcends the practical and obvious, and includes the associations of hidden meaning—is called a symbol.

It is the content of symbolism, together with the qualities of its patterns, that gives art the importance of a catalyst, of an integrator of values and meanings for the community. The meaning of a symbol for the individual gains objective validity—and thus reliability—only when this meaning is known to be shared by others. It may be said that in the act of recognizing a symbol the mind transcends its isolation and enters into community, just as one's innate rhythm does when it enters the rhythm of a pattern.

Symbolism in art is, of course, not restricted to painting. It contributes to the meaning of all art, and it is strongly active in sculpture, which uses subject matter as painting does. The attempt to reach "the real behind the real" through symbolism is both very old and very new in painting and sculpture, and when I speak here mainly of painting, I include sculpture and all other visual arts by implication.

Medieval art was full of symbolic transparencies: the earth was inhabited by angels and beasts as well as men, and the skies merged imperceptibly into heaven. The Renaissance and the subsequent rationalistic epochs discouraged such poetic irrationalities. "Imagination in art," says Courbet, "consists in finding the most complete expression for an existing thing. . . ." He also said, "Show me an angel and I shall paint you one." Until recently it was mainly the surrealists who tried to recapture the possibilities of symbolism.

These modern symbolists have great difficulties in reaching the modern mind. Only as children are we allowed the naïve freedom of imagination that enables us to see an airplane in an orange crate and a living baby in a rag doll. "After the age of twenty"—to quote from Dr. Lemaitre's lucid study, "From Cubism to Surrealism in French Literature"—"very few retain more than a dim, whimsical recollection of the fascinating realm wherein they spent their younger years. Then nearly all possibility of intense, spontaneous enthusiasm as a result of contact with the simplest aspects of nature is irretrievably lost. . . . Yet the Surrealists believe that in most of us the capacity for genuine enthusiasm is not altogether annihilated. Even if we allow our lives to be ruled outwardly by a rational and practical conventionalism, our suppressed mystic tendencies often find a safe refuge in the depths of our subconsciousness. . . . The purpose of Surrealism is to liberate from all shackles these supposedly rich and fecund potentialities of our inner being. We must grant them, say the Surrealists, absolute freedom and allow them to give us their message in its illuminating entirety."

All this runs counter to the attitudes that modern society has conditioned man to adopt. To break down these attitudes, surrealist painters have become propagandists. By unexpected juxtapositions of objects with incompatible and often unpleasant connotations, they hope to shock man out of his limitations. Some surrealists have been successful with their sensationalism, and some beholders, instead of awakening to new responsibilities, have derived a morbid pleasure from their work. The success of surrealism in establishing a viable symbolism, however, has not been great. This may be partly because surrealists, in their immediate aims at least, have not seemed very constructive, and also because of the pseudopsychoanalytical accent on sex in much of their work. The central difficulty of modern man lies not in sexual repression, but in the one-sidedness with which his rational faculties are socially coördinated and his emotional ones are not. By working with painstaking naturalism, the surrealists have addressed—and shocked—man only on the level of rationality, where symbols abound; they have not reached him on the level of emotion, where coördinating symbols are most needed. I think this misjudgment of aim more than any other shortcoming explains the failure of surrealism.

Man would make swifter progress toward a new symbolism if he could recognize the fact—implied in the early work of the Bauhaus school, and in the drawings and paintings of Paul Klee—that all objects and shapes continuously carry symbolic overtones, and that his occasional notice of symbolic meaning is not an accident but an essential part of his observation. Thus the lines of figure 24 are not lines only, they are also symbols. The vertical line, defying gravity, symbolizes uprightness and determination; the horizontal one conveys a meaning of passivity and relaxation; the slanting one, apparently falling, suggests activity. The three shapes of figure 25 are similarly fraught with symbolic content:

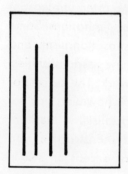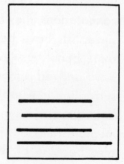

Figure 24

 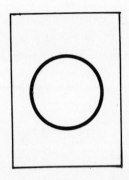 

Figure 25

there is violence in the first, serenity in the second, and finality in the third one. The fact that one cannot say whether this impression of finality in the cross derives from Christian memories, or from the canceling out of a vertical and active movement by a horizontal and passive one, illustrates the profundity of a symbol's power. In other words, the symbols are there. The possibility of developing them into a socially coherent symbolism depends on the development of a participatory attitude by both artist and public.

Paul Klee's drawing, "Migrant Fish," at the end of the preceding chapter (figure 23) illustrates this possibility. This drawing does not depict fish in the sense of illustrating their appearance: it rather conveys the idea of migration through symbols of fishlike movements. The integration of pattern and subject matter transformed into symbol that Klee realized in this drawing matches in this respect the accomplishments of the best artists of the past.

Beholder

Analysis of the pictorial medium and the separate considerations of space, color, pattern, and subject matter have not reduced the effort necessary to participate in contemporary painting—or, for that matter, in any work of pictorial art. However, although the task has not become easier, it has become clearer. The heightened awareness of the complexities of the medium gives insight into the potentialities of pictorial art. Description of two extreme cases shows the range of the relations between painting and beholder.

A work of pictorial art may function, artistically speaking, as part of the object that carries or contains it. Thus, its function would be to amplify and to differentiate the message of art expressed by the object as a whole. This kind of relation between an object of art and its surface art exists between the stained-glass windows and the cathedral. The creator of this kind of pictorial or surface art must feel himself instrumental in giving an amplification of the artistic content emanating from a truth that is vaster and more real than he himself can ever hope to create alone. His attitude toward his work cannot be one of the detached and specialized artist. He is no judge of the truth he is stating, because this truth is the very essence of his existence. He is, if he is a master, only a judge of his craft—that is, a judge of the means by which he achieves his statement. He will not sign his work, because he feels that it is not the artist, but the truth he has put into his work, that matters.

The beholder of this kind of pictorial art shares the attitude of its creator. He instinctively realizes that the security of his unitary living is of the same ethos and value that the artist has expressed in his work. Gratefully he accepts the windows and the cathedral as a reassurance of his faith. Since the truth of the values on which he depends is rooted in the form of society—or in the collective unconscious of the beholder and his contemporaries—he keeps the impact of the art with all his reason, feelings, senses, and intuition, and feeds the wholeness of his existence. Since meta-rational recognition is the major part of his awareness, he will receive the work of pictorial art in the rhythms of pattern and in the significance of symbols. Rhythm and symbol are the two elements of painting most closely woven into the cloth of society. The creative use of rhythm and symbol, both by the artist and by the beholder, maintains the unitary character of their society and strengthens its vitality.

The opposite extreme of pictorial art appears in the naturalistic easel painting. Here the relations between the artist, his work, and the beholder differ in kind from the ones described above. An artist may witness a hunting scene, and his feelings may be engaged by the horses, the sunshine, or the crowd. He selects a canvas of suitable size, together with the media readily supplied by modern technology, and notes down his observations as they appear framed in his field of vision. Naturally, since the artist's impressions are not as unselective as those of the photographic camera, his paintings will show deviations from the reality of the scene he has observed. According to his mood or his intention, he will have made his statement a little gayer or a little angrier than the subject matter itself.

The beholder who is interested in this kind of painting will approach it in the same manner as the painter approached the scene. He will be an onlooker, a private person of sensitive and trained feelings—a connoisseur. The impressions he is going to gather, he knows, will not touch the structure of his personal and social existence; for this structure, he feels, is anchored elsewhere—certainly not in the exhibitions of art galleries. Thus he looks forward to observing, at an agreeable distance and without personal involvement, the story the painter has depicted; and he relishes the comments that, by implication, the painter has cared to make. He will enjoy the hunting scene because he likes horses, or because the blue sky and the green grass remind him of a pleasant day in the country, or because he is interested in the commentary on the life of fashionable society the picture contains. He may find in the artist's comment a confirmation of his own private conviction that something is right somewhere with society; or, if he sees Hogarth's "Gin Lane," he will be privately convinced that something is wrong elsewhere with society.

Since in this example reasoned awareness is the main vehicle of communication between the artist and the beholder, it follows that pattern, rhythm, and the imagery of symbols cannot be very important. The painter and the beholder will rely in this case on the illusions of "real" space and "real" people, animals, and objects. Thus the particular takes the place of the common, the individual overcomes the social; the painter and the beholder have become lonely people.

This isolation prevails, not only because critical observation singles out, but also because whatever one observes is aimed at conscious recognition. Consciousness, as we know today, is not so much the driver as the one driven by forces at the roots of action of all men. Thus the beholder's recognition of the story in the hunt or in "Gin Lane" cannot influence the anxieties and answer the desires for guidance relating the beholder to his fellow men. At best the beholder will establish closer contact with the painter as a private individual whose work he appreciates and in whose life he is interested. This private relation, however, will not give the beholder or, for that matter, the artist any assurance of togetherness. I suspect that the opposite will be true; the preoccupation with easel painting will increase their loneliness. I suspect that the satisfaction they find in meeting privately—and perhaps only symbolically—a kindred soul will weaken their awareness of the need for overcoming the excessive critical detachment that forms the root of their loneliness and insecurity.

Between the two extremes of pictorial art lies the history of Western painting. Early easel painting, in keeping with the inquisitive spirit of the Renaissance, introduces the portrait and the landscape as a means of increasing the beholder's critical knowledge of reality. Easel painting during the Baroque offers the beholder, who is still securely anchored in the form of his society, the heightened awareness and reflection he craves for the consummation of his existence. With the disintegration of the societal fabric of the Baroque, easel painting develops the dissociated subjectivity of unrelated description known as Naturalism. It also develops Romanticism, the extreme, perhaps, of loneliness, in which the artist flees from an unbearable reality into the "long ago and far away" or into his private self. There he practices what E. M. Forster has called "internal dialogue" and, in many instances of morbid introspection, confounds the beholder, who finds himself confronted with visual statements without communication. Although many people vicariously enjoy this assertion of supreme egotism, "by this standard," as Anthony West says in a book review for "The New Yorker," "a scream is more significant and more real than a thoughtful statement." Having climbed steadily until it reached this stop, the indicator today seems to fluctuate erratically over the whole scale. In its leading representatives, however, painting shows promise of redressing the extremes of subjectivism by projecting statements of more objective validity. To the uninitiated beholder, this new departure offers an enigma. Trained to be an observer, he finds it difficult to assume the participatory attitude the new painting presupposes.

Incidentally, the changes in the beholder's attitude toward painting are reflected in the changing economic situation of the painter. An interesting sidelight to the history of painting is the fact that until the Renaissance most paintings were executed by retainers, and that during the Baroque most were commissioned. The nineteenth century saw the advent of the artist who paints primarily "for himself"—and then tries afterward to find a buyer for his wares.

Role of Painting

Present-day painting is characterized by two paradoxes. The proper correlation does not exist between historical methods of painting and the corresponding ways of beholding necessary for the proper appreciation of pictorial art. Consequently Medieval, Renaissance, and Baroque painting is seen through modern eyes—a procedure that has led to bewildering results. The second paradox derives largely from the first one. Painters today, being conditioned by the nineteenth-century concept that—mistakenly including historical painting—frames all pictorial statements in independent canvases, attempt to present their new ideas in antiquated modes. The results of this procedure merely add to the beholder's bewilderment.

I suspect that these paradoxes have developed through the habit of considering pictorial art only in terms of collections, museums, galleries, and art dealers. This habit has not developed without reason. Paintings, in contrast to works of architecture and sculpture, are easily moved and stored. In contrast to works of the so-called minor arts, they are easily displayed. Consequently, paintings became favorite collector's items, bought—through dealers and for inordinate sums—often as proof of social attainment and as sound investment rather than for their art. Later assembled in museums, these paintings, taken out of their context of place and time, tempt the beholder to interpret them as intended only for the kind of enjoyment he himself is having—a mixture of rational and sensual satisfaction.

Since the market in old masters is becoming exhausted, the canvases of more modern painters are treated in similar fashion. Dealers promote them, and collectors and museums buy them; and, following the example of the old masters, they too take on the character of investments. It seems inevitable that recognition in the inner circle of dealers and museum curators becomes prerequisite if the painter is to find a paying public. Consciously or unconsciously he fits his work into the established pattern. The gallery-sized oil painting becomes the vehicle for the communication of his ideas, because it has become the recognized currency for the transaction of art.

The average person cannot afford the prices asked for these paintings; nor does he have the space to hang them. Thus he comes to consider painting as a special interest, one that the layman does not need to understand. At best, he visits an occasional exhibit, reads an art magazine, or acquires a reproduction that rarely does justice to the original.

Possibilities of relating painting again to the processes of communal form are now becoming apparent. They appear, for instance, in recent changes in museum policies. Old-style museums—Frank Lloyd Wright has called them morgues—simply displayed their collections. More dynamic museums today are beginning to participate in community affairs. They have frequently changing shows of contemporary art, for which they try actively to educate their public. They strive to establish contact between their artists and their patrons. They encourage rentals and sales, and they often are instrumental in the commissioning of paintings, sculptures, and other works of art.

Other possibilities arise from efforts to find a new context for pictorial art. One such context is suggested by the growing demand for prints and reproductions. Linoleum and wood cuts, engravings, lithographs, etchings, and silk screens here offer an opportunity to replace the artistically unsatisfactory copies now being sold. Artists, by designing their work for a specific production process, could offer small and inexpensixe originals that, assembled between covers like books or phonograph records, would fit into the home and satisfy a great need for intimate and direct contact with art. Another context is suggested by a new typography in which rhythmically designed pages invite pictorial statements complementing the text and overcoming the limitations of naturalistic illustration. A third context appears in modern ceramics, in which some of the greatest artists today have availed themselves of the invitation to produce a contemporary pattern, symbolism, and décor. Yet another context—and perhaps the most promising—is offered in the new architecture, in which large uninterrupted surfaces challenge the muralist.

This suggestion of a new context for painting may not seem feasible to everyone. Those who feel that the main function of art is to offer the common form for the seemingly uncoördinated elements of human experience will find that easel painting is a particularly difficult medium through which to convey this form. On the other hand, those who feel that the value of a work of art rests in the reflection it casts upon the creative artist submit to a philosophy that had more validity during the Renaissance and the nineteenth century than it does today. Then man fought for his right to be himself against the compulsion of a petrifying feudal society or of a runaway industrial technology. He found his ideal in the great independent personality, represented by the "great artist" and symbolized in the "masterpiece." Today the rights of the individual are established. Man's interest is shifting, therefore, from the achievement of the individual personality per se to the consummation of personal existence through attachment and union with the whole life. Thus easel painting has had its historical importance in helping to develop the human personality. By going to the extremes of a socially amorphous individualism that was far more critical than constructive, easel painting has helped to clarify the necessity of a new integration. It is important today as an experience on which the new departure will be based.

Thus it would seem that painting is reëstablished as an expression of communal form as its suitable form-context is rediscovered. It is no accident that the emphasis on easel painting as a reflector of the independent personality has paralleled the decline of architecture—the art of common space—and that the rediscovery of participatory space and rhythmic pattern in painting at the end of the last century coincided with the reëstablishment of architecture as a living art. Paul Cézanne and Louis Sullivan were contemporaries. Their work heralds the inception of contemporary form.

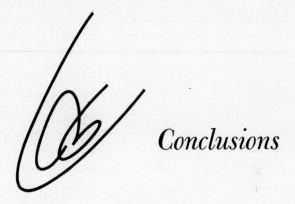

Conclusions

Function of Art

Within twelve years, at the end of the eighteenth century and the beginning of the nineteenth, both the École polytechnique and the École des beaux-arts were founded, dividing the training for the crafts of architecture into the two independent branches of engineering and design. This event marks the inception of the modern dichotomy between science and art. Both schools were undoubtedly intended to teach objectively valid principles—mathematics in the one, and classic rules of beauty in the other. Since that time, science has been able to maintain its objectivity and to prove its usefulness for society— at least to a point. Art has fared differently: during the Romantic revolution, it lost both its objectivity and its immediate usefulness for the community. Thus for the past hundred years, scientific thought has been the main element of continuity in the social

process, whereas art has become a considerably more discon-
nected series of private ventures into the realm of feeling. Today
the virtues of objectivity and responsibility for the continuity of
Western civilization are more conspicuous in science than they
are in the arts.

The approach to art described in this book suggests an approximation of science and art. It presupposes the existence of a
middle ground occupied by the whole man who, assured of the
reliability of science as far as it extends, is vitally concerned with
regaining the continuity and objective validity of art. One of
the means to achieve this goal is to connect the middle ground
of his position with art as it is now practiced and understood.
This connection I have attempted to show. The other means will
be to connect his position with the continuity of philosophic and
scientific thought. When he achieves this, he will have bridged the
gap between art and science and consummated the synthesis he
is seeking. It remains to be indicated how the unitary attitude
toward art may be approached by way of thought.

To understand the importance the whole man attaches to art,
it is necessary to recognize that rational man is an ideal, perhaps—a vision of certain schools of philosophy culminating in
the positivists of the eighteenth century—but that he is not commensurate with reality. This ideal exalts only one aspect of man—
reason—to the detriment of others; it neglects to appreciate the
integrated personality. Of interest here is the fact that during
periods in which such rationalistic definitions of man were advanced, art either stood in low esteem or it lacked creative power.

I have stated earlier—rather dogmatically—that unitary man
resembles a complex organization of impulses. Amplifying this

concept, his substance may be conceived as a differentiated will conditioned, with or without his knowledge, by surroundings, education, and heritage. These conditioning agents help to create a complex organism of more or less coördinated intentions. These intentions are partly within but mainly beyond man's rational control, for the energies that constitute and feed them are not confined in him. Like the ripples growing and reflecting around a stone tossed into a pond, the nucleus of will that is man links with and shares in larger systems of energy. These urges and intentions that do not end with individual man belong to an infinite existence including family, race, mankind, and finally—remotely yet directly—all life, all existence. The faculty of conscious awareness and rational control, which apparently sets man apart from other forms of life, seems to be only a secondary function of the vaster functions of life. It seems to be an organ of adjustment rather than of supreme management.

Man neither begins nor ends with his physical entity. His subconscious strata extend beyond him. Psychoanalytic studies have shown that even man's consciousness can be directed back to experiences that are his own and also those of prehistoric man. The fantasies of dreams, the miracles of love, the recurrence of spring are all evidence of a supraindividual union, of an all-embracing being. The instincts of self-preservation, on the other hand, the consciousness that assists these instincts, and the knowledge they induce, seem proof to man that he stands alone. The role assigned to him as his function in life makes his special self appear singled out and in contrast with the rest of the world. Man thus appears in a paradoxical position. He experiences a large unity, of which he sees himself as an organic part; and then again he realizes the independence of his own personality. When his egotism is dormant, he feels ties of common existence with nature, mankind, race, nation, community, and family; at other times he feels compelled to act as if he were responsible only to himself.

The longing to merge in the whole by relinquishing his precarious existence, or to sever the ties that link him to something beyond himself, the wish to decide for one or for the other, or to find a solution that follows the middle road—these occupy man's soul. It is to answer these questions that he most deeply desires a synthesis of guidance, warning, confirmation, and encouragement, and for which he uses his capacities to think, feel, and act.

The processes of the whole life are thus interrelated with all parts of a manifold reality. Yet none of the many fields of specialization—economics, politics, science, or religion—offers the nucleus for the synthesis man is seeking.

Economics is of no practical assistance. Recent history offers sufficient proof that economic man lacks almost all dimensions necessary to encompass the problems of unitary man. Production without fulfillment, to use John Dewey's phrase, abandons man at the point where assistance becomes most urgently needed.

Politics similarly offers nothing. Indispensable as a means, it is unacceptable as an end in itself. There has been more than sufficient proof that politics as an ultimate idea functions only through the prostitution of man's abilities.

Science offers greater promise. We have become accustomed to expect from science the solution to most of our problems. This expectation has been based on the assumption that the scientist has devised in the objectively controlled experiment a means to arrive eventually at some absolute truth. Two observations will warn us, however, against the belief that the experimental method of science will ever lead to more than partial results. The first one is that the problems of science seem to multiply with every problem solved. "Our points of contact with the unknown increase as the sphere of our knowledge expands." This constant increase in the number of problems tends to postpone indefinitely the moment when science will be able to integrate its evidence into the conclusive system it has led us to expect.

The second observation is more fundamental. It has been stated by Sir Arthur Eddington in "The Expanding Universe": "A scientist commonly professes to base his beliefs on observations, not theories. Theories, it is said, are useful in suggesting new ideas and new lines of investigation for the experimenter, but 'hard facts' are the only proper ground of conclusion. I have never come across any one who carries this profession into practice— certainly not the hard-headed experimentalist, who is more swayed by his theories because he is less accustomed to scrutinise them. Observation is not sufficient. We do not believe our eyes unless we are first convinced that what they appear to tell us is credible." It would seem that the scientific theories of which Eddington speaks are parts of a pattern of meaning. Science may verify our interpretations of meaning, but it does not create them. The a priori conviction that a certain fact is or is not credible decides its acceptance.

This may sound paradoxical, but when we compare the scientific convictions of any given cultural period with its attitude toward philosophy, we find science usually concerned with proving accepted or desirable theories. The Middle Ages would have been unable to accept the universe of relativity; we today do not accept the astrology of Kepler or the geography of Dante.

According to Ruesch and Bateson in "Communication," it has now been demonstrated "with rigorous proof that no system of statements [which is a good definition of science] can be self-contained in the sense of explanation of axioms and not self-contradictory."

These arguments suggest the conclusion that we cannot expect scientific methods of experimentation to produce the pattern of meaning for which we are searching. As for the scientific theories that advance science through the integration of complicated aggregates of knowledge—like Newton's or Einstein's or, most recently, Lancelot Law Whyte's, who shifts reality from fact to process—we must conclude that they come into being through intuition, an approach inaccessible via the scientific method in and by itself.

Turning to philosophy, we find here a discipline essentially preoccupied with questions of value and meaning. Throughout the history of Western culture, philosophers have repeatedly combined the results of scientific analysis with the experience of their time to present conclusive systems of thought. They have advocated the importance of ends over means, and have thus offered a pattern of integrated meaning. Yet philosophy, we find, is concerned with thought only: concepts form its subject matter. Philosophers, although admitting the theoretical character of their systems, have generally insisted that their teaching is meant as a challenge to action: they want to see their thoughts consummated in a way of life. The hope of the philosopher to see his thoughts thus realized rests on the assumption that to know is to act. Granting the possibility of such direct connection between thought and action in theory, we observe that it does not properly function today. With our lack of synthesis, with the schism of the soul in modern man, we find thought, philosophy, and wisdom on one side of the rift, divorced from action; on the other side we find action unguided by the insights of philosophy. Philosophy, in short, owes its effectiveness to concepts that have lost validity in the world of action. To arrive at a viable synthesis, we shall have to transcend the realm of philosophical concepts.

If we look to the roots of our civilization, we find in religion a force that transcends both action and thought. Religion has promised to supersede what Élie Faure has called the disintegration through knowledge with the integration through love. In Christianity, Western man possesses the formulation of a way of life that, by embracing both his finiteness as an individual and his infiniteness as a child of God, unites his polarities and makes consummate integration possible. Christ has shown us that this possibility can be a reality in action as well as in thought.

Religion, however, has not remained for Western man an imitation of Christ. In the preaching of disciples and reformers, God and man were torn asunder, as were mind and body. Instead of living in the communion with God and our fellow men that He had offered us, we became submerged again in the finite existence that Christ had exhorted us to overcome. Instead of shouldering the responsibility of sharing an existence of love, we regressed to the fear of God. Our desire to find ways of justification, and our attempts to understand intellectually what Christ had wanted us to know with the heart, pushed religion out of its position as the keystone of integration. Religion became an ideal of thought instead of a reality of attitude and work. Religion became a philosophical system and the domain of specialized theologians who, in the wilderness of their doctrinary disputes, lost for themselves and for their flock the path of the good life. It is for these reasons that established religions have failed to offer the pattern of meaning we need.

The example of Christ, however, transcends the rationalizations of the churches. Christ has shown us that the essence of religion is love—a love that cannot be exclusive ("For if ye love them which love you, what reward have ye?" St. Matthew, 5, 46). Beyond ourselves and our families, it includes our fellow men and all God's creation. Only to the extent that we accept the responsibilities of love do we recover the lost link between ends and means and close the chasm that threatens to engulf our very existence.

This responsibility for the persons and things that share our lives finds its expression in deeds—and deeds born of love do not and can not separate ends and means. We only have to consider our relations to the ones we love to know that responsibility is thought and deeds integrated in a way of life. Since similar relations tie us to other persons, as well as to the animal, vegetable, and mineral kingdoms, we should see meaning beyond utility in all our acts and in the tools that help us perform them.

The desire to fill our work with a meaning that transcends utility is the consummation of the love and faith of religion. It is also the force that retards and eventually reverses the trend toward disintegration by which we feel threatened. With the recognition of religion, we have found the force from which recovery springs.

We have also come to the point at which we recognize the contribution that art will make to this recovery. For the offering and partaking of meaning constitute the process of art, and art responds to our quest for synthesis in that its processes involve unitary man. As artists, we are not merely thinking, nor are we simply following emotional impulses inviting us to action; we are involved in a creative process that unites all our resources of body, mind, and soul. As beholders of art, we are similarly involved in a unitary complex of reactions culminating in experience rather than in specialized knowledge.

With this concept of art as a unitary process, we transcend what classic theories of art consider as their province. Instead of recognizing the fine arts, the content of which may eventually be applied to more utilitarian objects, we find a work of art to be any gesture, any utterance, act, or object that in addition to its utilitarian purpose carries an expression of meaning. Instead of seeing art as a group of aesthetic specialties, we envisage it rather in the form of a pyramid, the lower and broader tiers of which support smaller and higher ones. At the foundations of this pyramid are gestures of social intercourse. (Our "how do you do," for instance, is such a simple work of art; it is a gesture symbolizing acceptance of a code of behavior toward a person formally introduced.) Above these basic arts we find the arts of homemaking, entertainment, and fashion design. Beyond these, design for use gives symbolic significance to our tools for living, and architecture conveys meaning while meeting demands for shelter. Approaching the top of the pyramid, we meet arts that have become reflective, contemplating the heights to which the human spirit should ascend—the arts of sculpture and painting, of music and poetry. We must remember that this pyramid is meant to be seen not as a static structure but as a group of processes dynamically interrelated; the arts of the beginning not only support those of the end, they also determine and excite them and receive determination and excitement in return.

As this concept of art transcends classic theories, it also transcends—and here I approach the crucial point of this description—the possibility of proper definition. When we inquire into the nature of this meaning of art that goes beyond utility, when we ask how this meaning is conveyed and how it is consummated, we come face to face with an essential difficulty. It was found earlier that art is understood not through observation but through participation. Art addresses unitary man, which is another way of saying that art cannot be grasped by rational means alone. The quest for a definition, however, is essentially an undertaking of observation and rational analysis.

The nature of this dilemma is illuminated by Eddington when he points out in effect that no amount of explanation will make us laugh over a joke to which we have not responded immediately. Applied to our problem, this observation would indicate that no definition will bring us closer to a consummation of art because art transcends the resources of rationality. To proceed on our way to art, then, we also must transcend rational procedures. Instead of observing, we must participate. Instead of knowledge, we must seek experience.

Message of Art

Since art addresses the whole man, a work of art must constitute a whole. Man the specialist also, of course, approaches works of art in specialized ways. The connoisseur beholds them as sources of pleasure; the craftsman studies them for their techniques; the historian searches them for documentary matter; the psychologist scans them for revelations of their makers' personalities; the politician appreciates their propaganda value; and economic man marks their utility. These approaches to art find their rewards individually, because works of art contain them all. But these elements are only parts of a whole, and they cannot simply be added together to demonstrate the true significance of the whole. When a draftsman's triangle is taken apart, there remain only three wooden strips; the triangle itself has vanished, and its meaning is lost together with its unitary form.

233

Discussion entails analysis; and even when we consider what
Sigmund Freud has called the heroic belief in man's rationality,
we recognize that analysis in art means destruction unless it is
balanced in a process of synthesis. Vincent van Gogh was asked
one day to what school of painting he belonged. The painter
answered that he did not know; he knew only that he had an
assignment from God that he tried to fulfill. This assignment—
"from God" for a painter as consciously religious as van Gogh,
from some unknown power for others—is what I have called the
message of art. Since we cannot adequately describe the content
of this message in specific terms we must try by indirect means to
gain insight into its nature.

From diaries and letters of artists we learn that the process of
fulfilling their assignment begins with a state of tension, a tension
of which artists become aware under most diverse conditions. It
may awaken a poet from slumber; it may disturb a composer
while he seems to be doing nothing in particular; it may interfere
with a sculptor's working on a commission. A painter has thus
been interrupted while doing a routine portrait, a potter while
pinching a spout into a jug. Others may labor under the impact
of cumulative impressions inflicted upon them by love and death,
courage and despair, the wind, the stars, flowers, or perhaps
some quite rational idea that suddenly assumes deeper significance. As the creative moment approaches, the artist senses a
shape, a rhythm or a melody that, when realized with the means
of his craft, relieves him of that tension by embodying it in
what we later call a work of art. This externalization is not a
process of reasoning. Paul Claudel, as quoted by E. M. Forster,
describes it.

I do not speak what I wish, but I conceive in sleep,
And I cannot explain whence I draw my breath,
    for it is my breath which is drawn out of me.
I expand the emptiness within me, I open
     my mouth, I breathe in the air, I breathe it out.
I restore it in the form of an intelligible word,
And having spoken I know what I have said.

The artist thus leads us near the nature of his message, but he cannot explain it. He is engaged in the unitary nature of his work and cannot step away from the creative act for observation and description.

Let us observe, then, the artist at work. Selecting an instance of creativity far enough removed from our immediate situation to allow a panoramic view of the forces involved, we observe a village ironsmith who is fashioning a shepherd's crook—one of those outmoded implements we admire in our museums. Steeped in the traditions of his trade, the ironsmith has learned how to shape this tool. He knows its width, its bend, its function; he also has a conception of the proportions it is supposed to assume. Yet he does not make this crook strictly after a pattern; his knowledge is embedded in his imagination, which is subject to variation and change. So, while forming this tool, the ironsmith may be dissatisfied with the tradition inherent in its shape. A few variations in its appearance, some minor departures from the inherited pattern, so it seems to him, would perfect it—and he incorporates them in his product.

This may be all the ironsmith ever realized about the artistic significance of his work. He simply knew that he had done his work well because he felt that he had answered the challenge of the creative tension that was within him. It is equally true that to us—strangers looking over his shoulder—the meaning of what he has accomplished may remain hidden. The key to his message lies in the fact that the ironsmith has forged his implement not for us, nor for himself, but for the shepherds of his community. These shepherds, in possession of the traditions of their trade, material- ized the philosophy and the imagery that guided the ironsmith in his work. A shepherd not inspired by the meaning and the im- portance of his own way of life would not have been able to inspire the smith. He would not even have wanted to employ the smith. He could have chosen a gnarled branch of the required shape; it would have served him just as well as the creation of the smith—and he would have been saved the expense.

The crook, therefore, is to the shepherd more than a mere tool; it is a manifestation of his existence, a symbol of his way of life. The philosophy of this way of life is not the shepherd's alone; he shares it with other members of his community, and also with the ironsmith. Inchoate changes in this philosophy affect these people in their relations to one another, to nature, and to God—and a sense of uncertainty will accompany such transitions as long as their meaning remains obscure. The ironsmith, here a man of artistic faculty, feels these changes more strongly and more clearly than the shepherd. He also has the means of realizing the meaning of such changes in the form of his work. He is able to state, as Goethe puts it, not only what there exists but also what there ought to exist. Again, through his changed tool endowed with new beauty, the shepherd gains new certainty of his life's significance.

From the relations between the ironsmith and the shepherd emerges the idea of meaning in art—the message embodied in works of art expresses the form of a way of life.

Language of Art

The communication of the message of art depends on a vehicle, similar in function to the language used in communicating thoughts. In discussing the language of art, there are the same inherent difficulties that have caused the artistic message to be defined only by circumscription. "After having spoken I know what I have said"—the artist receives his inspiration, but it is not in rational terms; neither does he convey it through analytical description. The artist is totally engaged in his inspiration and in his expression, and he addresses the whole man. The vehicle he uses to convey his message reaches the mind and the heart of the beholder at the same time. The language he speaks is the language of imagery or symbolism. Since the work of art is a unity, its imagery and symbolism are not simply parts of it. The work of art as a whole may be symbol or image, and so may any element in it that happens to capture our attention.

If reason were the essence of art, the meaning of artistic images could be settled through analysis and deliberation. Since art, however, concerns the whole man, since the message of art is not addressed to reason alone but to will and emotion as well, the image must be of a complexity too great for any definition to encompass—the artistic image cannot be the result of reasoning. The imagery of art might be expected to develop and gain validity through its penetration into those deep psychological and biological regions of human existence where the message of art is conceived and consummated. The fish of the early Christians and the wheel as an image of the world were probably such images encompassing the depths of human experience. The eagle as an image of regal or national power, the scales symbolizing justice, in contrast, exist today on a level so rational that they are relegated to a place almost outside the creative arts. Similarly, Cupid, the Greek symbol of love, today lacks the directness of appeal to the whole man that an image of art requires.

In other words, the deeper and wider an image is rooted in the subconscious strata in man, the greater seem its potentialities as a vehicle of art—but the more difficult are its analysis and description; the more conscious and rational an image becomes, the thinner are the threads that tie it to creative art—but the better it lends itself to scholarly analysis and application. (It is for this reason that the more rational periods of art such as the Roman, Renaissance, Neo-Classic, and Constructivist have been of major interest for the art historian or for the eclectics.)

If, then, the image as the vehicle of the message of art is not established by deliberation, how else does it come to be selected? The artist at work has helped us to discover the meaning of an artistic message. He may also guide us to an understanding of his choice of imagery.

I repeat that his choice is not a deliberate one. Although there is the surrealist who declaims on the significance of the "found object," the significance with which he imbues it is actually a significance thrust upon him by some subconscious association. It is not he who transforms the object into a symbol; it is the symbol that crystallizes his vision. In this sense, the scheme of his imagery is suggested to the artist by his craft. The potter finds his imagery in the clay; the musician, the poet, the sculptor, the painter, the architect, or the dancer, each finds his adequate imagery in sound, language, volume, color, space, or movement.

Within his craft the artist faces further restrictions upon his choice. As an exponent of his civilization he will depend on images that are communicable, which means that they must have associations with knowledge that is to some extent established. The ironsmith who lived in a steppe country could not have fashioned a trident; his shepherds would not have understood the image and would have missed the message. If he lived in a shore village, the knowledge of his clientele of shepherds and fishermen would have been broad enough to appreciate both his trident and his crook.

These illustrations suggest that in a society of relatively static cultural pattern the artist's choice is severely limited; he depends for his imagery on what has been established for him by tradition. The wandering bards who delighted the knights and ladies of medieval castles with his ballads of the fights and quests of the knight-errant could not produce his rambling recital in the strict lines of a sonnet; the Gothic stonemason could not have suggested the erection of a Classic temple; a Baroque painter could not have cast his visions in the mold of stained-glass windows—their message would have been wasted because their imagery was inaccessible to their patrons.

Cultural patterns, however, do not remain static. They vary from day to day, and every new generation presents marked changes. It is in the realization of these changes that the artist's choice of imagery becomes a creative act. The public may feel dimly that a certain experience is no longer expressed adequately by a certain image that seems to have become sterile. The creative artist, seeing this condition more clearly and suffering by it more acutely, changes the image to restore its vital core. If he has not moved too far ahead of his patrons, his new image will be accepted. When certain arts are strongly active as formulating agents of society, the creative artist and the beholder of his work may be expected to be not too far apart in their interpretation of current imagery. Architecture—a very social art in the sense that it needs for its realizations the coöperation of an interested public—shows how closely the builder-artists have conformed with their patrons in the interpretation of changes in the imagery of shelter and space.

In other circumstances artists less preoccupied with the immediacies of their tasks may have moved too far ahead. Explanations will not offer them much assistance; it will take another generation to do them justice. The fates of Rembrandt, van Gogh, and Whistler are cases in point. When we ask today—as their contemporaries have asked before us—why Rembrandt introduces the imagery of light and shade, and why van Gogh conveys his message through the violence of his color, and why Whistler relies on the subtlety of his color harmonies (his contemporary Ruskin accused him of slinging his paint pots in the public's face), we meet the same impossibility of finding a rational answer as we have met in attempting to state the message of art.

The difficulties in elucidating the artist's choice of imagery are heightened when we observe that in times of transition the symbol often remains unaltered while its significance undergoes change. The human figure, for example, has served to depict gods and group ideals of heroes and saints; it has been used to portray the character of individuals; it has been the vehicle of shapes and surfaces of sensual and tactual interest. In recent times it has become the medium for the realization of moods, as with Lehmbruck; of structure, as with the Cubists; and of rhythm, as with Moore. Or we observe that landscapes have been foils for saints, as with Giotto; spatial echoes, as with Poussin; experiments with light, as with Monet; picture postcards, as with the naturalists; and images of rhythmic order, as with Feininger and Klee. None of these artists explains why he chose his particular imagery, and our quest leads us back to the need for participation.

Retrospectively, such entering into the artist's imagery seems to be no problem. When we take poetry, the most articulate of the arts, as an example, we have no difficulty in understanding in broad terms that after the heroes of Troy had ceased to be symbols of life, and after the spell of Vergil and of the poets of the Nibelungen saga had been broken, the unity of the poetic image disintegrated as national groups emerged. In Dante, Petrarch, Shakespeare, Donne, and Milton, we sense the lyricism of the Renaissance and the metaphysical intentions of the Baroque. After Goethe, the last universalist, made the transition, the poetic image becomes the expression of personal vagaries in the contemporaries of Wordsworth. Recently, there is a sense of return to a new integration, with the French symbolists, with Rilke, and with T. S. Eliot. Yet what we accept here as participation may be only a knowledge of the rightness of a poet's image as projected onto the ideas determining the cultural climate of his time or of the time his work foreshadows. What should give us pause are the difficulties that we encounter with the imagery of our contemporaries, and that other generations have encountered with the artists of their time. The French Impressionists introduced a new imagery, which for us today seems clearly the natural outcome of the then-developing scientific way of seeing. Yet, their still rather romantic contemporaries resented the new departure and could accept the creed—that a head of cabbage may serve as well as a vehicle of expression as a scene from the life of Achilles—only after they had become convinced that the emphasis in Impressionist imagery had shifted from the scenes depicted to the qualities of light conditioned by the painters' subject matter. Here, the critics helped. In other cases the difficulties of participation remained unrelieved by outside assistance.

To take an illustration from music, Beethoven, as Wagner and Schönberg later, encountered difficulties of communication because he enlarged the musical image with the introduction of new instruments, new chords, new changes of key. To his listeners, all human passion had previously been encompassed by the limited orchestra of Mozart and the harmonic structure of Bach. They did not feel that Beethoven had enlarged this image, but rather that he had destroyed it; and they reacted with bewilderment and anguish. Beethoven's compositions were simply not music until, through frequent listening aided by a change in the cultural climate, participation in his new imagery had become possible. We can form some idea of this predicament when we observe the bewilderment of friends of the ballet who cannot comprehend the shift from melody to rhythm apparent, say, in the compositions of Stravinsky.

In our difficulties with the imagery of today, there remains, of course, the argument that the artist, despairing of understanding and acceptance, has turned cynic and uses his freedom to scheme for the mystification of his audience in a sort of revenge. This argument has been advanced repeatedly in the past, only to be refuted later by a better understanding of the artist's intentions. It interests us here only because it illuminates the difficulty of participating in symbols that are not part of a generally shared language of imagery.

When the society in which the artist lives has the coherence of a common way of life, his choice of imagery will connect itself somewhere with images that have been established. Even when he is "progressive," there will be in his audience a progressive minority sufficiently large to spread the appreciation of his work. When the artist lives in times of extreme cultural differentiation and, unguided by his public, must rely on his own preferences, when artistic freedom arises in the sense that the artist is free to choose his own imagery—then participation or nonparticipation in his work by the general public becomes a problem. From this point of view, his freedom must be less of a blessing than it is a burden. Unless the artist finds an image that communicates itself sufficiently to invite participation, he remains in effect mute; and only a narcissistic satisfaction with self-expression or else heroic belief in the future will save him from despondency. The artist, in short, depends for his choice of imagery on the assistance of his public.

In all the arts, from poetry to pottery, the artist's choice of imagery is determined in considerable degree by the limits of experience or knowledge that the partaker of his work can be expected to reach. A basic image of common interpretation, a reliable core of communication, has to exist to enable an artist to impart his message. This image can be anything from the utilitarian shape of a tool to the subject matter in a painting or the rhythm of a poem as long as there exists agreement as to its meaning between the artist and his potential public. I have shown that certain images of common meaning pervade any given period of culture; they seem as much a part of culture as leaves are part of a tree. And the meaning and form of images within a given culture change only gradually, as the leaves of a tree change with its growth through the seasons. As long as society sees in art not a means of escape from the responsibilities of life but a form-giving agent for the purposes of life, men will insist on the integrity of such meaning. The discussions that are waged around contemporary art show the concern of society to possess an imagery of artistic communication.

The necessity of sharing an imagery imposes a responsibility on both the artist and the beholder of art. With historical works of art this responsibility rests with the beholder alone, since their creators are no longer alive. Since the artist has no control over his creative vision, at least in its decisive initial phase, all we can ask of him is to be aware of the traditions and tendencies active in the men of his era. This awareness will feed material into his work and extend his imagery beyond his own private world. The larger share of responsibility for the functioning of his imagery rests with the beholders of his work.

The beholder's participation in such processes should not be limited to interest in the artist's products. In asking questions about the artist's imagery, the beholder participates, of course, but only in a partial and passive way. Participation in the circumambient processes that lead to the artist's choice of imagery brings the beholder closer to the unitary process of art. It implies an awareness and a sense of responsibility for events of community and nature. Active participation in these processes will attune the beholder's mind to an appreciation of the imagery the contemporary artist uses and sharpen his senses for it. And since such participation implies an interest in the historical background of today's conditions, it will also open a way to the understanding of imagery in historical works of art. Once the beholder has grasped some aspect of the meaning of artistic imagery, his awareness of the conditions surrounding the creation of a work of art will supply him with the guidance that its imagery does not offer by itself.

The suggestion that we seek to understand the imagery of art through participation in the cultural processes that produced it— or in the recapitulation of them—may seem somewhat absurd to those who have not been led by their interest in art to the realization that the very existence of art depends on such active participation. The discussion of the language of art has offered, perhaps, the intimation that art does not fit into the old pattern of the active creator and the passive beholder. The realities of creative art suggest rather that the people assist the artist in bringing a work of art into existence. As Walt Whitman puts it: "To have great poets there must be great audiences too."

The magnitude of this challenge appears in its full proportions when it is seen as a parallel to the challenge of justice and law. Those unwilling to accept the responsibilities implied in Whitman's lines will maintain that they have an innate sense of beauty and that "there is no disputing about tastes." They ought to maintain equally that man also has an innate sense of justice quite adequate as a code of living. Yet history is replete with dismaying examples of how destructive of others this private sense of justice can become when it is not transcended by objective law. This law is not one man's opinion forced upon others; it is the expression of conceptions held in common. Legal order must satisfy the individual's sense of justice to be maintained for any length of time; it also must transcend this sense to make community function. The whole man expects to find such order not only in law but also in the form of art.